Cynthia Carbone Ward

How Writers Grow

A GUIDE FOR MIDDLE SCHOOL TEACHERS

FOREWORD BY Sheridan Blau

HEINEMANN
Portsmouth, NH

64230359

9-26-06

Heinemann
A division of Reed Elsevier Inc.
361 Hanover Street
Portsmouth, NH 03801–3912
www.heinemann.com

Offices and agents throughout the world

© 2006 by Cynthia Carbone Ward

The author and publisher wish to thank those who have generously given permission to reprint borrowed material:

Excerpt from "The Teacher" by Tom Romano. In the *English Journal*, 71 (March 1982). Copyright 1982 by the National Council of Teachers of English. Reprinted with permission.

Excerpt from "Morning Glory" from *Fuel* by Naomi Shihab Nye. Copyright © 1998 by Naomi Shihab Nye. Reprinted by permission of BOA Editions, Ltd.

Excerpt from "Introduction to Poetry" from *The Apple That Astonished Paris* by Billy Collins. Copyright © 1998 by Billy Collins. Reprinted by permission of the University of Arkansas Press.

(Credits continued on page 125)

Library of Congress Cataloging-in-Publication Data

Carbone Ward, Cynthia.
  How writers grow : a guide for middle school teachers / Cynthia Carbone Ward.
    p. cm.
  Includes bibliographical references and index.
  ISBN 0-325-00975-9 (alk. paper)
  1. English language—Composition and exercises—Study and teaching (Middle school).
I. Title.

LB1631.C38 2006
808'.0420712—dc22   2006006023

Editor: Lisa Luedeke
Production service: Denise A. Botelho
Production coordinator: Lynne Costa
Cover design: Catherine Hawkes, Cat & Mouse
Cover illustration: © Corbis
Typesetter: House of Equations, Inc.
Manufacturing: Steve Bernier

Printed in the United States of America on acid-free paper
10 09 08 07 06 RRD 1 2 3 4 5

Contents

For my father,
Saverio William Carbone,
my first and best teacher.
He knew what was important.

Foreword

Miraculous Writing and the Legacy of Tradition

As every accomplished writer knows, a good book, a good essay, a good poem is a miracle or feels like a miracle to the writer who produces it. That's because it seems to come from some place of inspiration and eloquence and wisdom to which the writer would not claim access by any act of mere will. Yet the act of writing itself brings one to such places as if by some gift of grace that feels to the writer beyond his or her conscious control. That's why writers in ancient times began their poems with invocations to a muse and why writers in all times have spoken seriously or half seriously or (now) meta-phorically of being visited by the muse. Moreover, while all good writing comes as a miracle, what seems to distinguish real writers from mere dabblers in writing is that real writers experience miracles with considerable frequency. And that, of course, is what much of the discipline of writing is about. It's about putting in your seat time, having access to strategies for helping yourself through the difficulties of the composing process, and persisting in the hard, challenging work that will make you available for the miracle when it strikes.

Cynthia Carbone Ward, no doubt, thinks of her book as a miraculous birth, though she knows better than any of us how hard and long she worked at it and how much it is the product of many years of thoughtful and some-times frustrating teaching, quite aside from a lifetime of apprenticeship as a writer (with considerable success as the author of prize-winning short stories and memoirs). Cynthia also knows from her own experience as a writer and a teacher how much intellectual and emotional and literary nourishment is required to nurture a writer or to cultivate the ground in which student writers will grow and develop. And that is the knowledge she shares in detail in this book, not just in the broad strokes of a giver of advice, but in the detailed plans and step-by-step descriptions of a good coach or of an experienced practitioner talking to other practitioners about the real daily work of teaching and of writing. And what she offers to all of us who are teachers and her colleagues she offers without a note of condescension or superiority, but as a colleague talking to colleagues she respects and from whom she is as willing to learn as to teach.

But as much as this book emerges from a miracle of composition, a lifetime of work at becoming a writer, and many years of reflective teaching practice in the classroom, which is to say, the personal and professional history of its author, it also emerges from a particular current of cultural history in the fields of literacy education and professional development for teachers, along with a parallel history in the field of educational publishing. That cultural history is inscribed in the careers of two key figures in education and educational publishing—James Gray, founder of the Bay Area Writing Project and the National Writing Project, and Robert Boynton, founder of Boynton/Cook Publishers, which in 1987 became a part of Heinemann publishing, the publishers of this volume.

In the summer of 1974 Jim Gray founded the Bay Area Writing Project (out of which grew the National Writing Project, now with 189 sites at colleges and universities in every state of the union) on two revolutionary principles: first, that the best teacher of teachers is another teacher; and second, that teachers of writing must be writers themselves. From these principles there emerged a new model of professional development for teachers, including a new model for inservice workshops in which an experienced and successful teacher (identified as a writing project teacher-consultant) presented to colleagues a hands-on demonstration of an exemplary teaching practice, requiring that the audience of teacher-participants actually produce and share some writing. Another unique feature of these workshops was that the presenter didn't merely demonstrate a successful practice, but framed that practice in a rationale or theory that explained its provenance, its purpose, and its place in the teacher's plan or curriculum for teaching writing over the course of an academic term or year.

These founding principles also gave rise to a substantial body of writing by teachers of writing from the Bay Area Writing Project and from the rapidly growing network of affiliated writing project sites sprouting across the nation. Not surprisingly, much of the writing of these writing teachers was about the teaching of writing and much of it took the form of the presentations these teachers were giving for colleagues, including step-by-step accounts of successful teaching practices and a rationale or theory accounting for the principles behind the practices and the place of each practice in a larger curriculum for teaching writing. Within a few years after the founding of the writing project, articles and monographs by writing project teachers began to appear in print available for the teaching profession at large in such publications as *California English*, the NCTE's *English Journal*, and beginning in 1979, in a series of "Curriculum Publications" published at first by the Bay Area Writing Project and later by the National Writing Project.

At almost exactly the same time that the writing project was developing its principles and practices under Jim Gray's leadership, Bob Boynton was deciding to retire from his position as an English teacher and head of the upper-school at the Germantown Friends School in Philadelphia and to establish his own publishing house (with a financial partner) to be called Boynton/Cook Publishing. Bob was, like Jim, a legendary teacher himself and an especially gifted teacher of writing and, like Jim, he also believed in the expertise of successful classroom teachers and in the importance of having that expertise shared beyond the walls of their own classrooms. He too was a writing teacher who wrote for his colleagues and for publication.

As a publisher and an educator Bob Boynton saw a great gap in the professional literature available for teachers and knew that what teachers needed were books written by outstanding veteran teachers who were reflective practitioners and willing writers. And he quickly realized that the Bay Area Writing Project and the burgeoning writing project movement nationally was a hothouse for nurturing the kind of authors he was looking for. With Jim Gray as his philosophical partner (and eventually his close personal friend), Bob quickly turned Boynton/Cook publishers into the world's leading publisher of books for teachers of the English language arts and most especially for teachers of writing—books written largely by classroom teachers themselves. Hence, beginning in the decade of the eighties, Boynton/Cook (and then, after 1987, Heinemann-Boynton/Cook) published such books as *Teaching Writing: Essays from the Bay Area Writing Project*, edited by Gerald Camp

(1982); and books by a number of other teachers affiliated with National Writing Project sites and related projects like the University of New Hampshire Summer Writing Program, including groundbreaking books by teacher-writers who were soon to become superstars in the growing constellation of expert classroom teachers who were reshaping the teaching of writing in classrooms throughout the English-speaking world—most notably, teachers like Lucy Calkins, Nancie Atwell, and Tom Romano. By the next decade, thanks to the influence of these seminal writers and the enabling work of Jim Gray and Bob Boynton, the paradigm of professional authority and professional authorship in literacy education had shifted and classroom practice in the teaching of writing and reading and literature was being continuously revitalized and transformed by a stream of books from Heinemann-Boynton/Cook by such classroom-based writers as Linda Rief, Maureen Barbieri, Kathleen Andrasick (Rowlands), Fran Claggett, Jeff Wilhelm, Regie Routman, Joni Chancer and Gina Rester-Zodrow, Carol Jago, Jim Burke, and Harry Noden—most of them writing project teachers and virtually all of them closely connected to some writing project site or parallel program.

Every book participates in a genre and a tradition, and the authors I have named and the model of professionalism and educational publishing developed by Jim Gray and Bob Boynton define the genre and tradition in which Cynthia Carbone Ward's *How Writers Grow* now takes its place. Cynthia was a gifted writer before she came to the writing project, but what the writing project gave her—aside from additional professional knowledge—was a new sense of opportunity and of professional responsibility to use her talent as a writer to write about her teaching and to share her teaching expertise with colleagues nationally through the publication of a book grounded in her own teaching experience.

Teachers who take up Cynthia's book will find it rich with ideas for the teaching of writing in classrooms, and wise in the attitudes toward writing and learning that it helps teachers to cultivate in themselves and in their students. They will also find in it an inspirational teacher they will want to emulate in her passion for teaching, her compassion for her students, and in her insistence that her students accomplish more as artists and intellectuals than they ever imagined they were capable of. Readers will also find here a writer worthy of their emulation, though they may not be able to (nor should they want to) imitate her uniquely graceful voice. It is a voice that is conversational yet precise, straightforward yet melodic, as if in song. And the song it sings is one that will lift all teachers to celebrate the opportunity they share to help students grow into writers who will be ready for miracles.

Sheridan Blau

Acknowledgments

My heartfelt thanks to the following special people:

Vickie Gill, *mia sorella*, for the essence of Chapter 3, but most of all for her unfailing friendship and support;

Linda Marie Smith, for her helpful reflections on teaching literature, and the enthusiasm and inspiration she provides daily;

Kelley Brennan, my dear friend and fellow traveler, for believing in me with such certainty;

Dorothy Jardin, for her eloquent counsel and the gift of her poems;

Miki Holden, for her insightful comments, keen eye, and good heart;

Jason Whitney, for finding time to talk to me even when he had twelve other things to do;

Jan Brown, Cornelia Becher Cadwell, Jennifer Levin, Ted Martinez, Eric Mortensen, Larry O'Keefe and my extraordinary colleagues at Dunn Middle School, for their musings, humor, and encouragement all along;

Bob Isaacson and the Gaviota Writers' Group, for a decade of writing and sharing;

Lisa Luedeke, for her epic patience and unwavering kindness;

the students and former students of Dunn Middle School and Vista de las Cruces, from whom I have learned so much;

and Monte and Miranda, my loves.

Introduction

I would rather be known for the things that I am good at, but the truth is, I am becoming famous for my inability to swim. It's a limitation that is impossible to deny or conceal at a middle school where the curriculum includes beach trips, surfing, and P.E. classes in the pool. One spring afternoon at the shallow end it became clear to me that it was my duty to at least get wet. For months I had been telling kids to push themselves, accept new challenges, and do what seemed most difficult. Being fearful and fifty didn't seem like a good enough excuse for not trying.

I immersed myself tentatively, a large terrestrial mammal in an alien element. And the wonder wasn't in the cold refreshing slap of it, or the shimmer of sun on aquamarine, but the circle of students that gathered around, instructing, encouraging, and supporting me. "Lean back and float," they urged, and they showed me how. "Put your face in the water! Hold onto the wall and keep kicking!" Isn't it funny how something that is so easy and natural to one person can seem impossibly difficult to someone else? It's a good thing for a teacher to remember.

But these were gracious instructors and benevolent graders. They believed I could achieve this, which gave me a feeling that I might. Even when I thought I had accomplished very little, they gave me credit for my effort and assured me that I had done well. What I wanted most was to propel myself across the pool and make them proud of me, but they were pleased just knowing I had tried hard.

And so, although I never actually learned to float, I left the pool feeling absolutely buoyant. I knew the scary startle of letting go and being new and that old sinking sense of simply not getting it, but I was lifted by the faith implied by others' encouragement, and by my own renewed belief in dogged effort. I saw in that moment that teaching and learning are not opposites at all, but two faces of the same fluid process, and depending on the play of light on the water, we glimpse one or the other in any given moment. I remembered in fact why I am a teacher.

Back in the language arts classroom, I've tried to hold onto my swimming pool epiphanies, and generally they seem to apply. Learning to write requires that we first splash around in the medium and overcome our fears. It requires practice and positive reinforcement rather than the intimidation of constant criticism. Teaching writing takes great patience, a singular sense of purpose, and maybe more than anything an outrageous sort of faith in one's students. Occasionally mine will surprise me with their interpretations or lead me to new insights, but often they will flail about while I feel hopelessly submerged or uncertain how to reach them. I don't think this is unusual for a writing teacher. I am sure that most of us wish now and then for something tangible to hold onto, even if it's just a few words of encouragement and advice, or some reassurance, perhaps, that we're not alone.

My intent with this book is to provide just that. It's the guide I wish I'd had when I first started teaching writing . . . and for all the times throughout the years when I felt overwhelmed by the enormity and ambiguity of that task. In *The Poetry Home Repair Manual*, Ted Kooser repeatedly mentions two fundamental tips about poetry, but they apply to writing in general: one, it should be accessible, and two, it should be written with an imaginary reader in mind. Following Kooser's advice, I've tried to make this a clear and usable book, and I imagined as my reader an earnest new teacher—or an experienced one—who needs a little boost, especially one who values the true and time-consuming craft of writing in an authentic, in-the-bones way, despite the continual interference of external pressures.

Indeed those external pressures are very real to us all, but we must not lose sight of our priorities. Conscientious teachers at all levels struggle daily with conflicting demands and expectations, particularly in the current political climate with its emphasis on standardized testing. In its recent report, *The Neglected R: The Need for a Writing Revolution*, The National Commission on Writing advocates nothing less than "a cultural sea change" in the emphasis and approach to writing in America's schools. The following passage from the report mirrors my own belief in the transcendent importance of writing:

> Above all, as students and young adults begin a lifeline of learning, they will find that writing is liberating, satisfying, even joyful. Writing is not simply a way for students to demonstrate what they know. It is a way to help them understand what they know. At its best, writing is learning. Writing competence builds confidence, which readily turns into creativity and fun, precisely what is most frequently absent from the policy discussions about today's schools. As a nation, we can barely begin to imagine how powerful K–16 education might be if writing were put in its proper focus.

Unfortunately, writing is *not* given proper focus. It is a complex and labor-intensive skill that too often gets short-changed in the chaos. You already know the end result: students are not learning to write well.

As for me, I am not an academic and I have no groundbreaking new theories to offer. I am simply a teacher who believes fervently that it's time to slow down, rethink, and invest the time and effort it takes to really teach writing. Toward that end I have gathered tools and tips that have worked well for me over the years, woven these together with anecdotal narrative and student examples, and offer it to my fellow teachers of writing in a spirit of friendship and support. I even believe that better test scores will follow, but that isn't the primary goal. (Sometimes you have to tune out the noise and focus on what matters, even if the noise sounds authoritative; that takes a little courage, but good teachers have courage to spare.)

I picture this as an airy book with plenty of room for you to wander, interpret, and improvise. I will refer you to other sources for more in-depth discussion of particular theories and topics, but in this book I try to focus on the quick hands-on quintessence. I have included my own creations and adaptations as well as a few sturdy ideas that have been around for a while, and I don't claim to have invented the latter, but maybe they'll be new to you. Those who are well versed in the literature often assume that everybody knows this stuff, but I haven't found that to be so. In any case, I thought it would be nice to have these activities and prompts conveniently compiled in one handy little manual.

Of course, it is possible to construct such a manual only because others before me explored the waters so much more deeply. Many dedicated and inspiring teachers, researchers, and theorists have contributed to my understanding and practice, and I am profoundly grateful to them all. However, I'd like to mention a few who particularly inspired me, starting in 1992, when I abandoned a career in public administration and enrolled at the University of California at Irvine to earn a teaching credential. There were several factors involved in my decision to teach, but the most salient was the death of my beloved brother Eddie, which left me with a different awareness of life's brevity and an urgent desire to do something meaningful in his memory. I didn't know what to expect from a teacher education program, but since I fancied myself a bit of a writer I particularly looked forward to the language arts methods class taught by Carol Booth Olsen, who surely has no idea what an important influence she was. It was in her class that I first heard writing discussed as a *process*, and she was an exemplary teacher herself. She made the invisible steps tangible, led us into writing of our own, and showed us ways to do this with our students. It was exhilarating to look at something I thought I already understood and see it in a whole new way.

In my first year in the classroom I discovered Nancie Atwell, whose classic book *In the Middle* was a revelation and a bible, albeit a daunting one, and while I never could replicate what she managed to achieve, I drew heavily upon her ideas about writing workshops, reading, and working with middle school kids in general. I thought then Nancie Atwell walked on water, but I have been even more impressed by her later reflections in which she admits to having gone from being a "creationist" to an "evolutionist" in her classroom: learning, adjusting, and "always beginning." I love that spirit, especially in someone who is already so exceptional.

That was only the beginning. Before long I came upon Peter Elbow's lucid thoughts about free-writing and evaluation. I read articles by James Moffett, who rendered knowable the inner workings of the essay; Donald Graves, whose insights revealed how writers develop; and George Hillocks, who advocated the teaching of writing as a reflective process. I also discovered the existence of the National Writing Project and specifically the South Coast Writing Project (SCWriP), its Santa Barbara manifestation. Here was a network of passionate professionals—experienced teachers who generously shared ideas, supported each other, and who themselves (sometimes timidly) loved to write. Project fellows present teaching ideas to their colleagues through demonstration lessons that model actual classroom practices. This is followed by reflection and discussion that encourages the development of theory. The SCWriP director, Sheridan Blau, is especially well known for his enlightening work on how readers make meaning from text. But even beyond his outstanding scholarship, Sheridan is known for the behavior he models as a teacher—his enthusiasm is legendary, and he has a beautiful way of seeing (and thereby eliciting) the best in everyone. Throughout his long career he has managed somehow to sustain an ongoing sense of surprise and wonder, often asserting that he learns more from his work as a teacher than his students could ever learn from him, and that tells you something right there.

I have long been an avid reader of books about writing, and authors such as Anne Lamott, Natalie Goldberg, Patricia Hampl, and Georgia Heard are mentors beyond measure to me. I have also had the honor of attending workshops led by Naomi Shihab Nye, whose insight, compassion, and poetry are fuel to us all. And long before I started teaching, there was William Stafford, the best friend I never met. I always loved the quiet eloquence of his poetry; I later rediscovered him as a teacher of writing whose ideas (in books such as *Crossing Unmarked Snow*) convinced me to give kids a little more space, to encourage rather than intimidate, and to allow writing time to be pleasurable.

Through SCWriP I was also introduced to theories of composition, literacy, and assessment, both classic and controversial, and I participated in classes led by superb teachers such as Bob Tierney (the writing process as discovery), Tom Romano (finding a voice), Patricia Lambert Stock (from experience to exposition), and Gabriele Luser Rico (crafting poetry through re-creations), among others. Who could have conjured up a more amazing collection of guides? I am grateful.

On the other hand, it would be misleading to say that I consciously think about all of this in the day-to-day reality of the classroom. In fact, I was very reassured when one of the finest teachers I know recently confided, "I love to read educational theory, but I am definitely a teacher of the chewing gum and baling wire variety—whatever works—and sometimes just whatever I can think of." I believe this is a lot closer to the truth for most of us. Of course we draw upon what we've internalized through our reading and experience, but teaching is interactive by its nature, and situation-specific. No matter how diligently we prepare our lessons, we are constantly responding, fine-tuning, and sometimes even shifting gears or changing destinations altogether. I certainly know some wonderful and accomplished teachers, but I can think of no perfect teacher who does everything exactly right. Teaching is highs and lows, epiphany and drudgery. There are days when everything seems to hum, and days when I wonder if it's time to switch to another profession. Mostly I just do the best I can and try not to lose heart. To the extent that I have teacherly wisdom, it has been hard earned and acquired over time. I am a kinder, gentler version of Cynthia today than I was ten years ago, far more patient with my students and more respectful of them as diverse and singular individuals. It's an approach that I advocate today.

Some of the suggestions I offer in this book may work beautifully for you, others may require tweaking, and still others may not be workable in your situation. Don't be afraid to experiment, and don't be afraid to blow it, either, because you'll learn a lot from that. I must admit here that almost all of my teaching experience, both public and private, has been in small rural schools, so I have not experienced the same challenges faced by those who work in urban contexts with broad cultural and language diversity and student loads that are triple mine. I acknowledge that reality, try to address it, and hope that this does not negate the book's usefulness. Implementation and assessment will certainly be more difficult, but I believe the fundamentals still apply, and I think we can find enough common ground to make this a worthwhile resource.

Chapter 1 of this book is about getting started, and that is often the hardest part. The hope is that we can lead our students gently and playfully to writing, helping them to discover a sense of the medium of words in all their dimension and possibility. Poetry makes an entrance early on as the topic of Chapter 2; I think it was Naomi Shihab Nye who pointed out that our first thoughts as little children—fragments and feelings and flickers of light—more closely resemble poetry than prose, and that seems logical to me. Chapter 3 is about writing for results—in particular, letters, technical writing, and persuasive essays—practical and purposeful applications. Chapter 4 focuses on the use of literature as a springboard for writing, and Chapter 5 is about memoir, a very sophisticated and personal form of reflection and self-discovery. Finally, Chapter 6 offers concluding thoughts on assessment and sharing.

Through it all, the most important factor is the spirit we bring to the work. It isn't possible to be perfect, but we can certainly try to be kind. Carl Jung expressed it sublimely:

> An understanding heart is everything in a teacher, and cannot be esteemed highly enough. One looks back with appreciation to the brilliant teachers, but with gratitude to those who touched our human feeling. The curriculum is so much necessary raw material, but warmth is the vital element for the growing plant and for the soul of the child.

Please allow this thought to settle in as we enter, for it matters more than anything, and most especially in writing, which teaches life and gives voice to the soul.

1 Finding a Way In
How to Get Started

I don't teach you anyway, I think,
just lead you like a scout master
and hope you'll dip your hand
into the brook—cold like no
tap water you've ever felt,

— TOM ROMANO

"I'm putting my heart and soul into this," said Austin. "In fact, I'm putting in a whole truckload of guts." We were in a sixth-grade writers' lab and Austin had chosen to respond to a prompt titled *How to write a love letter*. Kids focused on elements such as coming up with an appropriate salutation (the preference was for ridiculously extravagant terms of endearment) and even pen choices (a purple-glitter gel pen was recommended, and every *i* would be dotted with a heart). Austin intuitively recognized that a large part of the process was about getting in the mood, and although he had no particular recipient in mind and not much in the way of content, he certainly approached it with the proper degree of passion.

When it comes to writing, passion is a wonderful impetus. And while not every student is going to dive right in with Austin's eagerness, it is possible—even necessary—to create a climate in your class that is at least conducive to enthusiasm. How do you, as teacher, make that happen? It's a daunting task, particularly when many of your students, even by sixth grade, will have already decided with absolute conviction that they hate writing and stink at it. Facing a classroom of impassive and resistant children, you must somehow find an opening, lead them in, and remain present for them until they can navigate on their own.

It isn't as mysterious as it sounds. Granted—there is a wondrous and intangible gift called talent that is outside our control and inequitably distributed. But beyond this lucky blessing, the fundamentals required to create a writer can be distilled into five specific elements. When these are lacking, even talent may go unused and undiscovered. The good news is that as a teacher you have more autonomy and power than you might realize to favorably manipulate these five components.

1. *Exposure*: First and foremost, writing requires fundamental exposure to language through culture and socialization. Simply stated, the potential writer must have access to words, whether on the page or as spoken tales. There is no other way to learn the rhythm of sentence, the magic of metaphor, the way life translates into language and vice versa. There are those who grew up swimming in seas of stories, those with parents who read to them, those whose warm lamplit rooms were lined with books. Obviously, many of our students did *not* enjoy such advantages, but it is possible to adjust some for this lack. It begins with reading and recognizing well-written work:
- Share the poems you love, conspicuously savoring the sounds.
- Bring in stories and use them as springboards.
- Brazenly emote when writing is powerful and luminous, whether published material or student work.
- Present examples of good writing daily and help your students to connect it to their own experiences and imaginations. It's called writing from plenitude.

Figure 1–1 provides a few ideas and sources for words to share aloud.

2. *Environment*: Writing requires proper materials and setting. You will need to arrange your classroom in a way that allows separateness as well as community. In my room, students generally sit around a large U-shaped arrangement of tables for whole-class lessons and activities or when sharing their work with the class. They may pair off in corners to share work with peers or literally crawl under a table (we call it "down under") with a pencil and notebook to claim a private writing space. When students are writing, you should hear no sound but the scratching of pencil on paper, or perhaps the click of computer keys if students have this option available. As a teacher,

A Few Ideas for Great Listening

The fun is in discovering your own, but here are a few suggestions and sources. I try to find pieces that model good writing, inspire thinking, stimulate conversation, entertain, and/or help create a sense of community through a shared listening experience. Keep your audience in mind: I have chosen work that is accessible to middle school kids, appropriate, and short enough to be read aloud. As always, there is an element of personal preference here.

Ten Short Stories

"All Summer in a Day" by Ray Bradbury

"Werewolves in their Youth" by Michael Chabon

"Eleven" by Sandra Cisneros

"You Can't Just Walk on By" by Borden Deal

"A Day's Wait" by Ernest Hemingway

"Thank You, M'Am" by Langston Hughes

"The Monkey's Paw" by W. W. Jacobs

"The Gift of the Magi" by O'Henry

"The Tell-Tale Heart" by Edgar Allen Poe

"Growing Up" by Gary Soto

Picture Books

The Sneetches by Dr. Seuss

The Cello of Mr. O by Jane Cutler

Life Is Good: Lessons in Joyful Living by Trixie Koontz, dog

Inspiring Excerpts

Check out sharing a sandwich from *'Tis* by Frank McCourt, pages 201 and 202

Tom Joad's speech from *Grapes of Wrath* by John Steinbeck

Merlyn's advice to young Arthur in *The Once and Future King* by T. H. White

For passages from great essays, the series *Best American Essays* is filled with possibilities. Or, consider writers such as Bill Bryson, Garrison Keillor, E. B. White, or Bailey White.

Try playing some bits from the radio program *This American Life*: topics such as "How to Win Friends and Influence People" and "Kid Logic" offer amusing possibilities, but carefully prelisten!

Finally, Jim Trelease offers an annotated collection of read-aloud stories and articles for preteens and teens called *Read All About It*.

Figure 1–1

your role is either to write along with your students or to discreetly mill about, checking in with individuals who may be veering off task, stalled, or just in need of a nudge. Help your students to appreciate the gift of in-class writing time (which in a classroom context may range from three minutes to perhaps thirty) and to respect the needs of others. In addition to creating a suitable physical environment, you must remove psychological obstacles and create a writing classroom where kids feel calm and safe. This is largely a function of the behavior that you model and reinforce:

- First and foremost, treat your students with kindness and respect. (More about respect in a minute, from the students' perspective.) Every teacher feels irritated and impatient at times, but kids need to know that you are essentially on their side. Be an advocate, not an adversary.

- Show your humanity and sense of humor. It isn't easy being eleven years old—or sixteen. When a student is shy and nervous or completely blows it and wants to disappear, tell about a time that happened to you.

- Defuse negative attitudes. Some of this is basic classroom management technique, but it is especially important when you are trying to create a climate that is conducive to writing and creativity. We all know kids who turn to mischief or silliness when they feel inadequate or can't relate. Your challenge is to redirect that energy, help them discover the relevance or purpose of a task, and reinforce their brushes with success. Don't give negativity a platform or allow the wrong leadership to dominate.

- Instill a sense of community in the classroom. As John Dewey observed, "There is more than a verbal tie between the words common, community, and communication." Structure ways for students to get to know one another, respecting differences but recognizing similarities. One of my own friends and colleagues, Jan Brown, who teaches eighth graders, asks them at the beginning of the year to bring in a photo or object from home that tells the others something important about themselves. Elise, a former student of mine, told me that the professor in her college poetry class started the term by asking each student to make a unique statement about himself or herself. (Elise described climbing—and falling from—a certain oak tree and included the specific thought she had in the instant before she fell.) The basic idea: we're about to begin a journey together . . . and this is who we are.

■ Establish the expectations that within this community, students will listen attentively when peers read work out loud, and they will respond to what they have heard with appreciative applause and positive comments. Instruct and remind until these are simply the norms. Lead the applause.

■ After writing along with the students, share *your* work, too. Students need to hear your voice and vulnerability. You are modeling what writers do, so be consistent and authentic.

■ Find the time to conference individually with students about their work. Honor all genuine effort, and be sensitive to the difference between criticism and guidance. Allow kids their dignity.

■ Give students opportunities to write just for the sake of writing, and not always for a grade. Let them vent in the pages of their journals sometimes or riff about whatever is on their minds. Provide in-class workshop time for individual writing projects. Writing represents a kind of freedom, but kids will never know that if everything they do is investigated and judged.

3. *Practice*: A writer must write and write some more. A crucial element of your job is to provide appropriate writing assignments and opportunities to write. This may sound obvious, but it doesn't always happen. Lack of time is often cited as the culprit, but if you believe (as I do) that writing is a priority, you will drop something less important. Students should write in your class daily, even if it's just a journal entry, and they should generally have at least one substantial writing project in progress. You will offer prompts that help spark ideas, and use frames that suggest ways to arrange them. You will orchestrate experiences that stimulate, and present models that clarify and inspire. For most of us—adult or child—the initial blank page is nothing short of intimidating, but your role is to help prime the pump and get the process going. It is impossible to become a fluent writer without practice. Only practice will yield the desired level of comfort, the opportunities for fine-tuning, and a sense of what is possible.

4. *Positive reinforcement*: And practice should be accompanied by feedback, not criticism. I will consider assessment in a subsequent chapter, but for now I am talking only about guidance, suggestions, and encouragement. The fledgling writer needs positive reinforcement in order to acquire the confidence and desire to go further. Conversely, too much hovering and criticism at this stage of the game can cause a student to turn away entirely. Writer lost. As William Stafford observed, "Beginners benefit from impulse, excitement, motion, [and] trying out things without the menace of disapproval." Come to think of it, this is actually a lot more fun for us as teachers, too. I'd much rather approach my job (and my life) with a sanguine spirit, looking for good elements upon which to build and attending to the shortcomings afterward.

5. *Empowerment*: Ultimately, writers need a purpose, whether consciously or otherwise, and when the purpose is fulfilled, a sense of empowerment results. It's self-sustaining—the prize that keeps you going, that which may at last elicit a belief in oneself as a writer. Empowerment may assume the form of external success: it is a heady experience to evoke an emotion in an audience, effectively communicate an idea, or attain a tangible action as a result of one's writing. There is a sense of empowerment also in the personal catharsis of articulating one's imaginings or experience, of living twice. When your students begin to define themselves as writers and feel this sense of efficacy, they're in.

Getting Started

But the teachers don't give up.
They rise, dress, appear before us
crisp and hopeful. They have a plan.
— NAOMI SHIHAB NYE

I am writing this in September. The heat of the day has subsided, high clouds have rolled in above the hills, and there is a certain slant of light that hints of fall. School is still in its start-up phase. Even after many years of teaching I experience a sense of excitement and apprehension as a new year begins; I recognize the proverbial butterflies in my stomach, not unlike what my students are feeling as they look up at me with earnest eyes, all of them still wanting to please, hoping for a good year. We are the same in these yearnings. I pray that I will not disappoint them.

I am armed with the standard attributes: good intentions, sturdy plans, and an intrepid sort of optimism. I am teaching what is known in middle school as Language Arts class, but we might just as easily be in high school English. I believe ardently in the possibility that my students can become competent writers and might even enjoy writing, whether they know it or not. My challenge is to find a way to access these young people.

On the first day, I give each student a journal: black-and-white composition books with thread-bound pages, exactly like the ones I used when I was a schoolgirl. The journals will become vessels of thoughts, urns to fill with favorite words, even blue-lined fields on which to toss the seeds of ideas that may be worth developing. Occasionally the students will freely write whatever comes to mind; more often they will write to a prompt. (There is more discussion about journals coming up.) Today I want them to reflect about their experiences and perceptions of themselves as writers. "Write about writing," I say. "What kind of writing have you done? Is it something you're good at, or something that seems hard? How do you *feel* about it?" Afterward, we share our thoughts.

"I like writing fine," declares Justin, no doubt speaking for many, "as long as I can write about what I want and I don't have to go through a whole long process of correcting and redoing it." I appreciate his honesty but make no false promises, noting that I have never known work to appear spontaneously in a perfect final form. I also assert my stodgy belief that it is important to master certain types of writing. We will not skirt this reality, and when we get to that point I will try to explain why such assignments matter. But let's not make this sound medicinal. In this class, some writing *is* just for fun, there will be choices, and not all work will be graded. We need to play.

About Journals

We'll get to the playing in a moment; a few reflections about journal writing may be helpful first. I initially envisioned the journal as being a very private space and I encouraged students to write whatever they were feeling. Some swiftly took ownership of their journals in a sweet adolescent way, decorating them, naming them, confiding in them. Others doodled in them, or used them as catch-all notebooks, or misinterpreted our journal writing time as a small retreat from any kind of thinking, essentially scribbling gibberish. I speculated that this might be a variation on Natalie Goldberg's "wild mind" concept, and I even considered the possibility that there was value simply in the mechanical routine of moving pencil across paper for a few designated minutes. (Okay—maybe I'm slow to see what is obvious to others, but I earnestly look for the positive, and I'll try anything to get kids to write.) However, as time went on, it became clear even to me that more accountability and teacher intrusion were necessary. I have since tried to find a balance, not wanting to completely dominate the journal-writing process, and certainly not wanting to grade the journals, but establishing ways to ensure that this is a meaningful investment of our precious time. In fact, if I were completely honest with myself (and that is a requirement of the job) I have to admit that I had gotten lazy about this journal business, and kids take things only as seriously as we do. Here's what I concluded:

- First of all, don't dedicate the time if you don't see the worth of journal writing. If you do, then give it a fair chance: make it a regular routine, don't shortchange the process, and write along with your students. However, be cautious about proclaiming it a daily activity unless you can really pull that off. For me, ambitious dailies tend to fall by the wayside, which makes me lose credibility *and* implicitly devalues the activity. Every other day or even weekly might be more realistic.

- To reiterate a not-so-profound revelation: there does need to be some accountability, even here, but that doesn't mean grading. Tell your students that you will periodically collect the journals, and do so. The insights you gain will be helpful. React to some of the entries with your own written comments. Keep one eye on what's happening during writing time, even though you're writing too. And give kids the option afterward of sharing bits of what they have written.

- Provide specific prompts to get kids started. (This book offers several examples.) Sometimes students already have something in mind that they want to write about and it's nice for them to have the chance to do so, but many kids will just freeze if you ask them to write without direction. (I think I would too.) When longer writing assignments are launched, the journal is a fine place to brainstorm ideas, sketch out passages, and capture thoughts before they fly away. It is equally valid to use the journal for literature responses. Previous journal entries may also provide beginnings or inspiration for further writing. I refer to this as harvesting ideas.

- There should be something sacred about the journals. They should not be used as substitute notebooks or be crammed into backpacks, and with few exceptions, I tell my students not to take them home. If a student becomes enamored of journal writing (and that's a wonderful development) I suggest that he choose a blank book of his own and maintain a personal journal at home.

As you can tell, it has taken me some time to find my comfort zone here in order to preserve the spirit of journal writing while avoiding an "anything goes" mentality. Journals should offer students a kind of freedom, but within certain parameters. I just want to make sure through it all that I err on the side of encouragement over criticism. I have a fanatical desire that my students acquire a sense of writing as being something other than painful.

Playing with Words

So I guess the extreme opposite of pain would be fun. Before students learn to work effectively with words, they need to take some time to look at them closely, observing their colors and connotations. They have to dive in and splash around for a bit, dazzled by the light and sound that exist even apart from literal meaning. Many kids intuitively understand this. When I ask them to name their favorite words, they are seldom at a loss. The room is suddenly filled with words, random and rambunctious: *serendipity, twinkle, swish, chortle, hullabaloo, lascivious, haiku, shellac, finagle.* . . . Definitions are fairly irrelevant to these choices. It's mostly about how delicious they feel as they slip off the tongue, or about some interior associations unfettered by reason.

Given time, encouragement, and a model, most kids will stretch their imaginations and look at words in a different way, sometimes surprising even themselves with what they write. You might start by playing with word sounds and patterns. Ask your students to create chants—musical assemblages of random words they may string together for imaginary rituals or celebrations. It is an activity that is purely about enjoying the sounds of language. Nonsense words and rhymes are fun as well—Lewis Carroll's "Jabberwocky" in *Alice's Adventures in Wonderland* is of course a classic model.

Sometimes we talk about place names. (I have always enjoyed saying *Nova Scotia*. I like the way it almost rhymes and goes from scratch to softness and lets my lips twice form a circle.) As we stare more deeply into the wells of words, I share a passage such as this one from a story of my own about a young man who impulsively decided to move to Wyoming, a destination he knew only as a word:

> Greg had gone to Wyoming, a pastel-colored rectangle in the left half of the map. He didn't know a damned thing about Wyoming. He just liked the sound of it. "Wyoming sounds like a wolf beneath the moon," he'd said. "Like a lone man roaming." He was an unemployed tire dealer from Pittsburgh who could see upside-down mountains in a blue double-U, and perhaps that was his charm.

The excerpt opens up many possibilities for journal quick-writes. What do you see in the word *California*? *Chicago*? *Timbuktu*? Which of the images are based purely on the word's sound and appearance and which on concrete knowledge or association? What sensory details does your own name evoke? Describe the appearance of someone named, say, Oliver Pennington or maybe Edna Getz. Or choose a word such as *Tuesday* and take a peek at its physical characteristics and personality: to me it is thin and anemic, pale green, always disappointed. Students have fun with this and enjoy sharing the results, both comical and seriously sensual. Years ago a sixth-grade girl name Clara stared deep into the word *summer*, licked and even bit into it, then leaned back and wrote the following:

> Summer tastes like a luscious plum dripping with sweetness and almost overripe. It is the sun beating down upon you as you lie in the tall grass under a tree. It is the sweet smell of honeysuckle climbing up an ancient fence. Its touch is the kiss of a light breeze rippling the grasses as if they were waves. Its sound is the drone of a lazy bee, slowly drifting from flower to flower.

Dallas chose *strawberries,* a specific and concrete noun, but he clearly savored his small journey:

Strawberries: the red blood of a dragon with white dots and a green stem. I would have in my room a whole garden of them. The little red cells of a dragon that is asleep. So sweet and watery and cool . . .

Be open to various interpretations of these admittedly imprecise prompts. They may be sparkling journal rivulets that go nowhere in particular, but it's okay to get wet and have a little fun. Play comes before work here, and don't ever be convinced that it is superfluous. This is the stage at which students may shed the dread. These initial sessions are about exploration and discovery, not critical evaluation. There will be plenty of time for serious business— I promise. Here are ten more starters, perfect for quick-writes in a journal . . . and the permutations and possibilities are endless:

- Before you even opened your eyes that morning, you could sense that it had snowed. How did you know?
- Open up a battered old trunk that has been in the attic for decades. What do you find in there? Describe its contents in great detail.
- Describe and compare the hands of a farm worker or an auto mechanic with those of a princess or a pianist.
- What does morning smell like?
- She didn't exactly say so, but it was clear she didn't like you. Why were you so certain?
- Consider the pros and cons of peanut butter. Describe it first as something nutritious and good and then as something disgusting.
- Describe an incident involving a banjo, an old sea captain, and the color orange.
- Describe as many kinds of rain as you can think of . . . or as many kinds of quiet.
- Think of something you're good at. Explain in detail how you do it and how you feel when it all comes together.
- List seven things that are wrong with school. (Then see if you can come up with seven that are right.)

The Sensory Walk

Another good start-up activity for a writing class is the sensory walk. Carrying a notebook and pencil, students walk around the campus in silence, collecting details of sight, smell, sound, and tactile stimuli. Upon return, they share what they have noted. It's fun to offer recognition to the person with the longest list of observations, or the most unusual. The compilation of everyone's contributions results in an evocative, multidimensional picture of the school at a certain moment in time. In middle school we use this to create a collaborative poem in which an opening line such as "I know campus on a Tuesday morning" unfolds in a listing of the characteristics of the place, laden with evocative detail. Students also use this format to write small individual paragraphs or poems describing something they know very well—Saturday soccer, the school cafeteria, or a family dinner, perhaps. One sixth grader, for example, focused on the sounds of her house in the morning, gathering auditory observations of her mom arguing with her sister, the news on television, her dad flushing the toilet, and her cat calling for food.

The idea is to encourage students to more keenly observe the world, to see as writers do, and then effectively communicate their vision and experience to others. A variation on the sensory walk is the "sit"—in which the area of observation is limited to a fifteen-foot radius around the student, and the written description zooms in, detail by detail. A small area encompasses the universe.

Don't be disappointed when students return with unsurprising reports about leaves rustling and birds chirping. It's a good moment to point out that while these are often-used phrases, they are also excellent examples of onomatopoeia. (And take heart: it is unlikely that the chirping of the birds would have been noticed had the opportunity not been provided. I call it a victory.) You may also be rewarded with wonderful observations about the dew-beaded cobwebs right outside the door; the shift of sun and shade upon the hills; the murmur of math-class voices; the smells of cut grass, coffee, and shampoo; and, as one sixth-grade boy recently noted, "the great humming noise of the silence that sits behind everything."

Being a Writer

One form of play is pretending. Since we want our students to think of themselves as writers, let them start off by imagining that they are. I borrowed this idea from my colleague Dorothy Jardin, who teaches creative writing at the high school, and assigned it to my sixth-grade students in lieu of an introductory autobiographical piece. Here is the prompt exactly as I presented it to my class, but there is nothing precise about the assignment, and many variations are possible:

YOUR BRILLIANT WRITING CAREER

You're amazing! You've just published your eleventh book and your publisher wants you to submit a fascinating publicity piece about yourself for a magazine.

- First of all, invent a pen name. Use your imagination.

- Now you are going to invent a life. Where were you born, and where do you live? What books, people, and experiences have influenced you? Who is your favorite writer?

- You'll have to tell what kind of books you write. Science fiction? Contemporary novels? Children's stories? Historical fiction? Mysteries? Romance? Fantasy? Some other type?

- Tell about your work habits. When do you write and where do you go to write? Early in the morning in a little beach bungalow? Or late at night, in your Greenwich Village flat, as the neon lights from the bar across the street cast their red and green glow onto the wall? How long does it take you to finish a book? Do you drink lots of coffee and type all through the night or chew on your pencil and get up every few minutes to see what's in the fridge?

- Your books are so popular you've become a celebrity. What is your life like now? Where do you live? Have you met any famous people? Is your latest book going to be turned into a movie? Who will star in it?

- What do you like to do in your free time? (Be as wild and creative as you like.) Do you have any pets, peculiar habits, unusual interests, favorite possessions? Anything else you want to add?

Have fun with this!

The purpose of this activity is to stimulate writing and to encourage your students to creatively imagine a creative life. As an assignment, it is intentionally freewheeling and the work it generates would be difficult to grade, but it will reveal much about your young writers. I can already guess the first two questions your students will ask, so let's get them out of the way. They want to know: *How long does this have to be?* and *When is it due?* (I would put money on this. Tell me if I'm wrong.) These are practical and intelligent questions in the competitive, grade-oriented context that is school as your students have known it. They want you to cut to the chase, quantify, give a clear beginning and a clear end, and provide a formula for the product. They are uneasy with process and open-ended prospects. I suggest you arbitrarily declare that four "good" paragraphs should suffice as a minimum and ask for a final version a week from today, allowing some time for them to work on it in class. Let them start immediately.

Fascinating developments will unfold. Some students have fun right from the start just coming up with their pen names. Julia became Courtney Giggles, a mystery writer from Virginia, and Luke decided he would be Adrian Von Shnickerfoot, who lives in London with his Scottie dog, Willie. Emily immediately pictured herself writing contemporary fiction while married to Orlando Bloom, who would star in the movie version of her book. Aidan had to know first if it would be okay if he were a screenwriter for full-length animated films. (Why not?)

Some students will systematically go through answering question by question of this prompt as though taking a test. A few are simply baffled by the whole prospect and wish it would go away. Many will do the bare minimum and others will delight you. You will find you are privy to some interesting revelations about how your students approach the task of writing or how they imagine others do. You will see, too, that some of your students do not yet know how to craft a sentence or organize their thoughts. The assignment will not be graded, but you have permission to be vague and elusive about this fact going in. (You will, however, give your students feedback. They *want* to know what you think. More about that in a minute.) This will be the first piece of writing in the portfolio collection of each student's work for the year. Think of it as a snapshot of the start and a springboard for setting some goals.

As I have stated, this particular assignment is not graded, but it is essential that you give your students feedback. In my comments, I always start with the positive elements– and there *will* be some positive elements in every piece of work, no matter how inadequate it may initially seem. In some cases, the most positive element might be that an attempt was made to do the assignment. It is your duty as a teacher to find something of value in the work and help counter the view many students have already formed that writing is a relentlessly discouraging ordeal. Be gentler than you think you need to be. To paraphrase Hippocrates, we must first do no harm.

That does not mean overlooking ways that the writing could be improved. I list these after the positives, usually limiting them to two or three suggestions at this stage, lest it seem overwhelming. I look at each submission individually but I am also cognizant of common patterns that may lead me to topics I should emphasize with the class. For example, I notice the tendency of many students to open with "hi"—because they honestly don't know how to start— and most pieces end somewhat abruptly. I identify these as points to focus on throughout the year. (In fact, it's consistent with my own experience in crafting essays: beginnings and conclusions are the hardest to parts to write.)

However, if I had to name the most frequent shortcoming of these and other student pieces I have read over the years, it would be that they are too brief. Much of the guidance and instruction I offer my students will therefore be on how to sustain and develop an idea. (Of course I understand that brevity has its place, but not right here.) Students must learn to write adequate paragraphs in which an opening sentence is followed by several sentences that support, explain, illustrate, or develop it. One tried-and-true way to promote this is by asking questions left implicit and unanswered in the piece. Students expand their thoughts by answering your questions.

Student samples of "My Brilliant Writing Career," along with my comments, are provided on the following pages. Other than spelling, which I corrected, the samples are exactly as they were submitted to me.

KATIE CADOO
by Katie

Hi. My name is Katie Cadoo and I was born in Kalamazoo on April 12, 1979. I never liked writing until I was 14. I was 18 when I started a book and 20 by the time it was published. Now I am 25 and I like to write detective stories for young adults.

I live on the island of Madagascar. I live in the deep isolated parts of the rainforest in the tree tops. My house, as you can probably guess, is a tree house! It is very open and breezy and there aren't many doors to shut ideas out. My windows are permanently open (the weather is always perfect) and the animals are always welcome. I love to hike around in the rainforest looking for ideas. When I write I listen to the animals and the sounds of the forest around me. They give me good ideas.

One of my favorite writers is Kate DiCamillo. She wrote *Tiger Rising*, *Because of Winn-Dixie*, and *The Tale of Despereaux*. Her writing is very deep and emotional. If you love tigers (like me) don't read *Tiger Rising* because it is very sad.

I am currently working on a series about a ladies' detective agency that travels around the world. Right now I am working on book number two and the characters are in Costa Rica to solve an age-old mystery. The mystery is about a ship that sank (no one knows why) and every lunar eclipse a ghost ship, sailors, and a captain come out to sail the seas again!

Dear Katie:

What a wonderful start! Your work shows imagination as well as a sense of beauty. I love it that you chose to live in a tree house in Madagascar where the windows are always open and animals are welcome. I think there is poetry in the line "there aren't many doors to shut ideas out." And you didn't just say you're working on a mystery: you actually outlined an intriguing plot—I'd want to read that book!

You have a voice. I feel as though a real person comes through in your writing. And you also have a sense of fun. Even just choosing to be Katie Cadoo of Kalamazoo shows spirit and playfulness. I appreciate that.

You obviously read the writing prompt I gave you and responded to it carefully. You write in complete sentences that have a nice rhythm, and you organized your work into paragraphs.

Here are some things that you could work on:

The opening paragraph of an essay can be the hardest part to write, but it is also very important because it sets the tone for the rest of the piece. There is no need to say hi. Jump right in. A good way to start is by giving your reader a colorful image or anecdote, and then you can back-pedal with some of the dry facts. You do grab your reader's attention with that delightful pen name, but other than that, your first paragraph has a lot of dates and numbers with nothing solid to hold onto. And you leave your reader wondering: What happened when you were fourteen that made you finally like to write? What was your first book about?

You've written the minimum of four paragraphs, but they are generally rather short. The most satisfying paragraph is the second one. Can you see why?

You already have many strengths as a writer! Good for you, Katie!

PENELOPE SPOTS
by Moraya

Hi. My pen name is Penelope Spots. I was born on August 17, 1985, and started publishing books when I was 15.

When I was 11, I met J. K. Rowling and she inspired me for my career. She is also my favorite author. I, like her, write children's fantasy books. I have met many other famous authors and have their autographs but I won't name them now.

When I write I usually sit at my kitchen counter and things stroll into my head. I always write at night because I like to be active in the day. One of the things I love to do in the day is to walk in the park because the random things that I encounter help me to think of ideas for my books.

My life is filled with autographs and photos. Now I live in San Francisco and always love to have breakfast on Main Street. I have 7 pets, 3 dogs (a lab, Bennie, a long-haired Chihuahua named Nicky, and a Brussels Griffon named Gabby, 2 cats named Bubo and Sally. I also have 2 house trained miniature ponies, Mattie and Sparkles.

I love to ride horses and I cherish my pets dearly. I have 3 friends that write with me 2 times a week and we share ideas together. I have one particular habit. I always drink chocolate milk when I write in the nighttime after dinner.

Only one of my books is going to be made into a movie so far, *Rush Across the U.S.* It is about a girl that can speak to animals and her horse gets kidnapped and she travels across America to get him back, but that's not all—you have to read it! The star in it will be Natalie Seminar and the horse star is her own horse Blue Fire.

I hope I get to meet you readers soon. (I'm doing a lecture in New York on Tuesday) and you read my publications.

Dear Moraya:

I like the way ideas "stroll" into your head. It seems to me that's what happened here. I think you're off to a terrific start. Here are some great things I noticed about your work:

You followed instructions. This is neatly typed, uses complete sentences, and is organized into paragraphs.

You invented an unusual pen name and interesting details. Your personality comes through. (Penelope sounds like a real animal lover!)

And Rush Across America *is an interesting idea for a book.*

Two things to work on:

Let's think about other ways you could have started and ended this. Your first and last paragraphs are too short. For example, instead of starting with "hi" you might consider giving your reader a quick snapshot or scene—maybe of Penelope at eleven years old meeting J. K. Rowling.

Give more specific examples and details. For example, it's too easy to say "random things" or "I won't name them now."

JONATHAN PIERCE
by Kai

My name is Jonathan Pierce. I was born at my great-great-grandfather's house in Africa. I wanted to become a writer because I loved to read and write when I was a kid and make up little stories. My teacher loved my stories and encouraged me to write a book. I write books about fantasy and myth, stories that are exciting and nerve-racking both at the same time.

Once I got out of school and on my own, I bought a place in the country. The place kind of seemed similar to where I was born. On the nights I didn't write I would lie on my bed and wonder what would happen next and what to write. On the nights I would write I would sit at my wooden desk and fan myself with some bits and scraps of paper. Most recently I took to looking out my window every few minutes drawn away from my writing. After staring out at my little garden I would get up and go make myself some tea.

I now live in New York in a hotel hiding from the many reporters and cameras that are now looking at me wherever I go. I'm still writing another book. When I have the free time I go out to the outskirts of the city and walk around seeing everything either buzzing, fluttering or flopping around, imagining that one day none of this would be here just cars houses and people, so I consider myself lucky to be around before it's gone.

Dear Kai:

You've written a lovely piece! Your writing is clear and elegant. I love the details such as the wooden desk and staring at the garden and making tea. I wonder what you see in the garden. Can you take your reader there? And I'd love to know more about the stories you write. Any details?

This a little on the short side and I'd like to see you write more. Your last sentence about the creatures "buzzing, fluttering or flopping around" is very beautiful.

I think there is a theme hidden in here—something about yearning to connect with nature and your concern about human impact on the natural world. Maybe you can explore this idea further in other writing this year.

I look forward to reading more of your writing, Kai. I'm proud of you for such a good start.

"My Brilliant Writing Career" is particularly well suited for reading out loud. Humorous fabrications are easier to share than personal revelation, so students feel less vulnerable presenting these invented lives. In our class, we organized an impromptu television show called *Meet the Authors* with the students as celebrity guests. They were surprisingly eager to get up in front of the room to read their pieces, gratified when they garnered laughter or compliments from their peers. Hearing the work of others read aloud also gives students an opportunity to observe variations in the way an assignment is interpreted. They appreciate the imaginative flourish of a classmate, for example, or perhaps notice that they wrote far fewer words than other kids. Finally, it is a good moment to point out that reading your own writing aloud permits you to hear how it sounds and flows, and there is something satisfying and necessary about that. (In my own writing, I consider oral reading an integral part of the process, the time to catch gaps or dissonance or simply savor the segments that hum.) The culture you create in your writing class should be one in which students listen respectfully and appreciatively to the work of their peers and feel safe to share out loud. "My Brilliant Writing Career" is an excellent point at which to begin this aspect of the socialization process.

A Few Final Words on Respect

Sharing one's work out loud, even a whimsical fantasy piece such as "My Brilliant Writing Career" takes a certain degree of courage and generosity. There are those confident kids who love to perform, but many others find the prospect daunting. I wish I could offer an easy recipe for creating a climate in which students can take risks and feel comfortable sharing their ideas with peers, but it doesn't translate into a simple process. In my own experience, the ease or difficulty of achieving this and the degree of overall success have varied from year to year. The bottom line, however, is mutual respect, and this always begins with the example set by the teacher. Several years ago, I decided to come right out and ask my sixth-grade students to tell me how a teacher should behave in order to inspire their respect and encourage a healthy atmosphere for learning. I found their responses to be helpful, insightful, and occasionally quite charming. Here are a few, and it seems to me they would apply in any classroom, no matter what the subject area:

- I respect a teacher who really tries to help someone improve.
- I respect a teacher who listens to my ideas, who listens to me . . . a teacher who has time for me.
- Have fun but be a little strict. Give us two chances at things. Don't forget that the things you say mean a lot to a kid.
- Don't lie. Keep your word, and if you say something, don't change it.
- I would look for a teacher who treats everyone the same and congratulates them on their work.
- I respect a teacher who gives a lot of help to her students and always explains good [sic] if they don't understand about something.
- I respect a teacher who does not break promises, and someone who is very loving and cares a lot.
- You should respect the student before they will respect you. If the student never receives compliments, only criticism, it is hard for the student to respect you.
- Things that make me respect a teacher: not a hypocrite, pays attention to her students, tries very hard at their job, does not insult students, is firm but not mean!
- A teacher should lay down the rules from the beginning and should never show that he favors one student, even if he secretly does.
- The thing that would make me give respect to the teacher is if she gave me a little respect back. I don't want a lot of respect— just a little.
- Be nice, but sometimes be strict. Not too strict.
- Mean what you say. Also, don't try to act like a kid!
- Be nice. When people are nice, nobody wants to get in trouble with them, and they want to be nice back to you.

- Give kids some breaks after long writing periods. Do some hands-on stuff from time to time. Be funny and nice, but stay a little strict.
- What makes me respect a teacher is when he follows through! Also, I like it when he likes kids and has fun with the class while we are learning. I don't respect teachers who don't like kids—why did they become teachers?
- I would respect a teacher if she were strict and meant what she said, but at the same time, be nice and joyful.

Granted, being "nice and joyful" isn't always easy, but there's a lot of genuine wisdom here and a few themes clearly emerge: Mean what you say and follow through. Establish a track record of honesty, fairness, and consistency. Be "strict" but not inflexible. Have a heart and don't be afraid to show it. These are core values in the kind of culture that should prevail in your classroom. But don't expect quick results, gratitude, or unanimous buy-in. Someday your students will realize how much you loved them and how hard you tried. Or maybe not. It doesn't matter. When you do your best, you respect yourself.

Share What You Love

When I say you are creating a culture and community in your class, I mean it quite literally. When students come through your door, please let them enter a world where words are valued, where writing is celebrated, where kindness is the norm. Writing is an elemental expression of our humanity, and that renders exceptional the place where it is taught and nurtured. Rise to the occasion. As a teacher of writing, you are in a unique position to introduce your students to art, music, or literature that inspires you. Read your class a short story whose message is a catalyst for written reflection, whose elegance makes it a paradigm of the craft. Have a poem always at the ready. Be human and accessible; share stories from your life, and tell them well.

I have a small overnight suitcase from the 1940s with brass latches that make a loud satisfying snap when I undo them. I used it for sleepovers in my early teens, but it's the type of luggage a well-dressed lady may have carried on a train once, with a satiny lining of midnight blue and a mirror on the inside. It holds a small collection of random, irresistible remnants from my life: beach glass, a broken doll, a New York City subway token, a tarnished medal from a long-ago science fair, an expired passport, a feather, a stone from Mt. Vesuvius. I refer to it as my storytelling suitcase because its contents provoke questions, evoke memories, and suggest odd ideas for poems and journal writing: What do you like to collect? Have you ever won anything? Where have you traveled? Did you once have a favorite toy? Describe the best gift you ever received. List what you have lost or broken.

Or bring in your high school yearbook—few artifacts are more fascinating to your students. When I tell a story about a disastrous high school date, my students clamor to see what Stanley and I actually looked like. Exclamations along the way about short plaid jumpers or hair teased into bizarre beehives segue into amusing themes such as "My Favorite Outfits" or "A History of My Hair."

Once I may have thought of this as self-indulgent, but now I see it as generosity of spirit. Use your good judgment, of course, but share your excitement. It is contagious. Show your vulnerability. It is familiar. And encourage students to bring in a treasure of their own. Whether it's a ticket stub from the Flaming Lips concert, the collar a beloved Lab wore, or a well-loved book that once was a refuge, it is all material for remembering, sharing, and writing. Photographs, too, are rich with possibilities—ask kids to write from a snapshot that vividly brings back the details of a special day, or to muse about the image of a relative long gone. When your students begin to discover their own stories, be one who listens. Feel honored by their reciprocity. You are building a climate of trust and enthusiasm. If the door opens to a warm room, some of the kids will wander in.

Draw Upon Your Own Experience

The earliest awareness of writing in my life is indelibly associated with memories of my father, who was an artist with words as well as paint. He painted murals, boughs of tender heart-shaped leaves, peacocks, clowns, and exotic flowers, even on the ceiling. I remember the smell of the casein paints, oily sweet dollops from silver tubes in colors like burnt umber, crimson, and cerulean. In his speech my father possessed an ornate incongruous eloquence forged from a bilingual background, hard streets, and sad stories, and an innate sense of poetry that no one could have taught him. On many nights, tired from work and still wearing his paint-freckled overalls, he sat and helped me with my homework compositions. He showed me how a sentence could became more satisfying if it followed its thought all the way through. He reminded me to end each essay with a flourish and gave me a thesaurus filled with words like a box of assorted chocolates. I sometimes wondered if I would ever be able to write a composition without my father's help, but his loving guidance took root in my head and in time I developed a voice of my own.

In fact, the best thing I ever wrote was a note on loose-leaf paper that I left for him on the kitchen table. I wished him good morning and told him I loved him; then I drew a penciled daisy by my name. He turned the note over and responded in kind on the back. Many things happened in the rush of time that followed, some of them hurtful and terrible. I learned, to borrow Austin's phrase, that it takes "a truckload of guts" to live a life. But I remain at the core of me the same earnest girl who wrote that note on loose-leaf to her dad, and I know with certainty that the words we exchanged are still current.

So maybe it is no coincidence that I now teach about letters and love and respond with ridiculous sentiment to declarations of passion and curiosity, especially from children. The act of writing is laden with meaning and memory; to teach writing is to teach life. (It occurs to me that the math teacher may feel this about math just as the science teacher believes it of science, but this in no way diminishes my conviction.) Writing mirrors existence, changes it, invents it. If you are to be a mentor in imparting this power to your students, you must do so respectfully. Please forget external voices for a moment, and put aside the lists of standards and measurable objectives—these are makeshift attempts to quantify the sublime, well-intentioned targets, but not your true purpose. Your students must first become comfortable with the medium. Be authentic and patient, and come from a good place in your heart. If you do not alienate them now, you have greatly increased your students' potential to achieve the tasks in those state-issued inventories.

Above all, do not neglect the writer in yourself. It has been said that those who cannot do, teach, but the truth is closer to this: those who *do*, teach best.

Recall your own attempts to discover your voice, your tentative forays into expression, the moments when you believed you were a writer, the times you fell silent. I still have a cherished bit of paper with my father's dear familiar handwriting, and I am profoundly grateful that I had the good sense to write down what I was feeling rather than keeping it mutely to myself. Perhaps I intuitively knew that writing is communication, the link between souls, the way we transcend time.

2 The Light in the Language
Looking into Poetry

or walk inside the poem's room
and feel the walls for a light switch.

— BILLY COLLINS

I know an eighth-grade teacher who was criticized by a parent for "wasting so much time on poetry." It makes me sad that poetry has become something that needs to be justified and defended, and yet it is, despite its being the ultimate written expression of human experience *and* the form in which we encounter the purest pleasures of language. But it isn't hard to see the origins of the disdain. Many of us can recall classes in which poems were analyzed to death or scholarly discourses that left us with the impression that poetry was an esoteric realm we could not truly enter without proper laborious instruction. And what would be the incentive, anyway, for doesn't poetry also have the distinct disadvantage of being useless in the practical terms that our schools and culture emphasize? So it isn't at all surprising that many view poetry as extraneous or painful.

But resistance dissolves when you read the work of fledgling student poets such as Mackenzie. Although she was a particularly talented seventh grader who loved to write, I doubt she would have so eloquently expressed her feelings had a teacher not been willing to "waste time" on poetry. Mackenzie's family moved with such frequency that she had grown to dread the sound of packing tape "screeching away from its roll" to seal the cardboard boxes of her memories. Here are a few lines from a poem she called simply "Leaving":

> I see the moving van and know my entire world is about to start over.
> I feel like water.
> I seep up into the air from the hot sand,
> form into a circular gas high up in the atmosphere,
> then drop thousands of feet.
> I'm always leaving.
> I fall so fast from the sky that when I hit the ground
> my heart is scattered in every direction.
> Once I am happy in my new location I leave again.
> When the sun comes out, I evaporate like water.
> I'm gone.

Or consider Jared, a seventh-grade boy who lived on a cattle ranch and wrote poems filled with colorful cowboy themes. This excerpt is about a rodeo participant waiting to be called for his ride:

> . . . my life passes before me,
> the farm in spring, just after cutting time,
> the dry sweet smell of corn stalks, carried by the wind,
> little Johnny with his plastic sheriff's badge and two Winchester cap guns,
> the loose floorboard at the back of the closet
> with the little tin safe and its rusty lock . . .
> the big screen door always open to visitors or weary travelers passing by,
> and the familiar smell of cigar smoke in the office.
> As I sit here waiting for my name to be called
> I think about my life and how good it was.

Finally, meet Billy, a long-ago sixth grader who struggled in school and had about him the aura of a waif. Sustained writing tasks were intimidating to Billy, but he enjoyed trying his hand at short poetic forms with specific rules and patterns, such as *diamante, cinquain,* or *haiku.* One day he decided to write a haiku about the afternoons he spent at his grandpa's house. It may not be the right number of syllables or in quite the prescribed format, but Billy felt that this was something he could do, and in my view he succeeded:

Tired all the time
boring, drowsy, slow
folding our blankets

Billy moved away, and I soon lost track of him, but I kept these lines because they spoke movingly, as the right words, spare on a page, can. To me, they evoke an aching sense of loneliness and monotony, and there is something surprisingly poignant about the small simple chore of folding blankets. It is that one detail, the single image, which makes all the difference.

Why You Should Take the Time

Each of these poems (and hundreds more) is its own compelling case for including poetry in a writing curriculum. But I offer the following points to more explicitly spell out the rationale:

■ Poetry is a way for kids to voice their feelings and fantasies, to create a space in which to be silly or serious, defiant or heartbroken, connected or alone. Where else are your students going to do this? As American anthologist and poet Oscar Williams wrote, "Anyone who knows how to love, or to suffer, or to think, anyone who wishes to live fully, needs and seeks poetry." It is impossible for me to fathom a writing program that does not encompass poetry writing and appreciation—and not just as an isolated unit, but as an integral part of the curriculum and a lifelong refuge.

■ Poetry gives students a chance to experience the sheer pleasure of language, to think metaphorically, and to play with sounds, images, and rhymes. Through poetry, students discover and savor the visual, tactile, and emotional dimensions of words and acquire a heightened sense of their grace and power.

■ Poetry presents opportunities to unleash the imagination, unfettered by mechanics. For those who find the essay form daunting and constrained, poetry is an invitation to break a line at whim, discard punctuation, and transcribe the meanderings of the heart. This is not to say that poetry demands no discipline or structure, but in the early explorations I would suggest that such considerations be relaxed or put aside.

■ Aside from the appreciation and creation of poems as such, forays into poetry help kids to become better writers in general. Student poets become more attuned to the rhythms of sentence, the nuance of word choices, and the power of bravely writing what one means.

Exposure to poetry is a lifelong gift to your students. Those who appreciate this art form will have found an enduring source of comfort and pleasure. "The magic," says poet Edward Hirsch, "lies beyond the words." It is in the link that is created between souls, the momentary glimpse into another's perception, the stirring recognition that you have been found.

Beginning

Start by accumulating an assortment of poems to read to your students. Factor in the age and life experience of your audience and be prepared for the reality that some of your most beloved choices will yield indifference and bewilderment. I have read poems with my voice cracking and my eyes welling with tears only to gaze upon a sea of blank faces, some distracted by the clock. Ah, yes. I too was once young.

But don't be discouraged; you will learn what works. "The Highwayman" by Alfred Noyes is a wonderful classic to read aloud to middle school students, or try "The Cremation of Sam McGee" by Robert Service. And sixth graders in particular can't get enough of Shel Silverstein, a delightful and accessible beginning. As for me, I can still recall the enchantment I experienced as a child reading poems such as "The Lamplighter" and "The Land of Counterpane" by Robert Louis Stevenson. Sadly, I don't think many children are exposed to such wonders nowadays.

Move on to some of the deceptively simple poems of Emily Dickinson ("I'm nobody. Who are you? Are you nobody too?"), the intriguing word play of e.e. cummings ("be unto love as rain is unto colour . . ."), the alliterative and sensual imagery of Elinor Wylie ("I shall go shod in silk, / And you in wool, / White as a white cow's milk") or the kindhearted eloquence of Naomi Shihab Nye ("There's a place in my brain / where hate won't grow. / I touch its riddle: wind, and seeds."). Not "up" on poetry? Try Billy Collins' *Poetry 180* or Garrison Keillor's *Good Poems*, or check out americanpoems.com or

PoemHunter.com, online resources that will take your breath away. A phenomenal resource for both poems and what to do with them in the English classroom is *A Surge of Language: Teaching Poetry Day by Day* by Baron Wormser and David Cappella. In addition to using poetry as a vehicle for teaching grammar, vocabulary, and other language skills, poetry is presented as a reflection of human experience and an impetus for higher-order thinking. "Each person's life forms a thread that links poems," the authors write.

As you gradually create your own anthology, you will discover there is a universe of possibilities. I've listed fifty of my own favorites right here to get you started, and it was hard to limit myself—I'd probably come up with fifty different ones if I did this tomorrow. Several of the following poems are well known and others simply small delights that caught my fancy at one time or another. Some are quite profound and a few just sound delicious. In any case, I don't think any of these are beyond the appreciation capability of middle school children, even if they don't always get every word:

"Ailey, Baldwin, Floyd, Killens, and Mayfield" by Maya Angelou
"Happiness" by Ray Carver
"Incident" by Countée Cullen
"On Turning Ten" by Billy Collins
"maggie and milly and molly and may" by e.e. cummings
"The Brain—is wider than the Sky" by Emily Dickinson
"'Hope' is the thing with feathers" by Emily Dickinson
"I'm nobody! Who are you?" by Emily Dickinson
"There is no frigate like a book" by Emily Dickinson
"Nothing Gold Can Stay" by Robert Frost
"The Road Not Taken" by Robert Frost
"Snow" by Nan Fry
"Knoxville, Tennessee" by Nikki Giovanni
"Those Winter Sundays" by Robert Hayden
"A History of the Pets" by David Huddle
"Mother to Son" by Langston Hughes
"The Negro Speaks of Rivers" by Langston Hughes
"If I Could Put a Curse on You" by Paul Janeczko
"In the Basement of the Goodwill Store" by Ted Kooser
"The Leaky Faucet" by Ted Kooser

"The Jumblies" by Edward Lear

"God's World" by Edna St. Vincent Millay

"Living with Children" by Jim Wayne Miller

"The Dog" by Ogden Nash

"Great Things Have Happened" by Alden Nowlan

"The Highwayman" by Alfred Noyes

"One Boy Told Me" by Naomi Shihab Nye

"Shoulders" by Naomi Shihab Nye

"Someone I Love" by Naomi Shihab Nye

"Wild Geese" by Mary Oliver

"Annabel Lee" by Edgar Allen Poe

"The Raven" by Edgar Allen Poe

"Richard Cory" by Edward Arlington Robinson

"In a Dark Time" by Theodore Roethke

"My Father Is a Simple Man" by Luis Omar Salinas

"Elephants Are Different to Different People" by Carl Sandburg

"Fog" by Carl Sandburg

"For You" by Carl Sandburg

"Sunsets" by Carl Sandburg

"The Blind Men and the Elephant" by John Godfrey Saxe

"The Cremation of Sam McGee" by Robert W. Service

"Winter" by William Shakespeare

"How Poetry Comes to Me" by Gary Snyder

"Oranges" by Gary Soto

"Being Young: Eleven" by William Stafford

"Choosing a Dog" by William Stafford

"The Lamplighter" by Robert Louis Stevenson

"Animals" (from "Song of Myself") by Walt Whitman

"The Eagle and the Mole" by Elinor Wylie

"Velvet Shoes" by Elinor Wylie

"I do not understand the power of poetry to transfigure," writes Bill Moyers in his book *Fooling with Words*, "but I remember the first time I experienced it." He talks about four high school English teachers who took time to read their students the words of Blake and Shelley, Byron and Keats, Tennyson and Shakespeare. "Looking back," Moyers concludes, "I realize they simply believed in the magic of poetry's music and sought to expose us—even the tone-deaf among us—to the pleasure of listening to 'the best words in the best order.'"

Finding Meaning

Naturally, you'll sometimes talk about the poems, but don't overtalk. I recall that the poet Eve Merriam compared prose to poetry by saying that prose demands its words to mean what it says, while the poem simply smiles mysteriously, and somehow its words must say what it means. Confronted with a Mona Lisa smile, we must resist the temptation to overanalyze and reduce to its component elements what is so much more than the sum of its parts. It is better to ask than to instruct. Were any feelings or memories evoked? Do certain sounds appeal to the ear? Are there images or phrases that linger? Is there something in here you can relate to?

I certainly respect the words of my colleague Jason Whitney, an outstanding high school teacher and a writer himself, when he says: "A poem is *not* anything you want it to read. There are only a certain number of plausible readings, and there *is* such a thing as a misread." On the other hand, I don't believe it is necessary that everything be rendered crystal clear. I have always favored Carl Sandburg's definition of poetry as "the opening and closing of a door, leaving those who look through to guess about what is seen during the moment." I think it grants us permission to leave a poem with some ambiguity intact.

High school and middle school students are particularly attentive to the poetry within the lyrics of their own music, and this provides an interesting avenue for exploration. My seventeen-year-old daughter, Miranda, once played me a song by Rilo Kiley called "The Good That Won't Come Out." It starts out "Let's get together and talk about the modern age" and leads into this refrain:

> It's all of the good that won't come out of us
> and how eventually our hands will just turn to dust,
> if we keep shaking them.
> Standing here on this frozen lake.

My first impression of the song was that it was a cautionary tale about all the intrinsic goodness that fails to find expression in overt acts. However, Miranda experienced it more optimistically as being about the good inside of a person that nothing could wash away. She found support for her viewpoint in the very tone of the music, which starts out quiet and builds into layers, defiant and celebratory. She reminded me, as well, that hammering out a decisive interpretation for every word diminishes enjoyment of the music—a pretty good poetry lesson right there. (But I recently had the unusual opportunity to ask Jenny Lewis, the writer of this song, which interpretation was intended. Her response? Both.) I suggest you invite your students to bring in music whose lyrics they appreciate. It enables you to initiate conversation about poetry in a way that gives your kids some footing. I know one teacher who even asks students to compile a CD soundtrack for their lives and to reflect on their choices. It is a revealing and enjoyable project.

One of my most memorable encounters with poetry took place in an eleventh-grade English class, circa 1967. The poem was about Buffalo Bill, written by e.e. cummings, and I can still recall the feel and smell of the purple inked mimeograph sheet upon which these words were typed:

> Buffalo Bill's
> defunct
> > who used to
> > ride a watersmooth-silver
> > > stallion
> and break onetwothreefourfive pigeonsjustlikethat
> > > > > > Jesus
> he was a handsome man
> > > > and what i want to know is
> how do you like your blueeyed boy
> Mister Death

I had never seen such a poem. There was something shocking about its brevity, its irreverence, its stunningly abrupt and candid address of death. I was used to hunting for deeper symbols embedded within text but here was a poem too spare and bold to hide anything, and it left me reeling. All in a moment a dazzling man on a silver stallion becomes defunct. Gone. Justlikethat. But what exactly did it mean? "Look at your own reaction," my wise teacher said. "I think you get it."

Catching Poetry

As Jason warns, it *is* possible to misinterpret a poem, but poetry is meant to be *experienced* first and analyzed only secondarily—and that initial experience requires a "right brain" kind of receptiveness. Poetry is, after all, as much about sound and texture and feeling as it is about literal meaning. An interesting technique for helping students to catch the essence and spirit of a poem is to ask them to arm themselves with imaginary nets, listen with eyes closed, then sweep the nets through the aftermath and see what phrases, images, and feelings linger. Students should jot these down and follow them to fragments and thoughts of their own. It will take some practice before they get the hang of this. Read the model poem as often as desired.

Next, instruct students to steal a line outright to start a poem of their own, or they may head somewhere new along a path strewn here and there with words randomly harvested from the model poem. But don't assume that kids know how to arrange poems. They tend to write in a paragraph format because that is what they know. Afterward, you can point out ways to break up the lines, and show them how variations can shift the focus, emphasize words, alter rhythm, and transform the overall picture. Remind them that none of this is random to a poet; each word and line break represents a conscious choice. But they will only learn by doing it. (The "found poetry" activity in Chapter 4 is also a good beginning activity for getting this across.)

Eighth grader Lizzie heard a poem (whose title and author I have sadly lost) that began with the line, "It is dangerous to break a round thing." This evoked a theme of circles that led her, as you will see, back to the fact of her Grandpa John's death:

It is dangerous to break a round thing.
The globe you gave me and said, "You will travel the world someday
and here is your start."

The checkerboard we played on with the round pieces designed so perfectly.
The coaster beside your chair with a "J" engraved.
The raspberry tootsie pops we ate so slowly,
trying to see how long we could go before a lick.
The shiny gold ring on your long left hand.
the round rug in front of the denim blue couch,
your face so full of light, and never a dark moment.
The round medallion strung from your neck that shined its bright light.
But now you are gone, and I am without.

Time for a Rhyme

I used to insist that kids avoid rhyme in the early stages of poetry writing, but I now think that rhyming is a fine game to play at. (One girl wrote about "an armadillo sittin' on his porch gettin' a daily scorch" and I was hooked.) Although forced rhymes dilute meaning, rhyming provides an enjoyable challenge, a sneaky way to stretch vocabulary, and an introduction to formal rhyme schemes and meters—and some kids simply can't resist it anyway. Besides, prohibiting rhyme would have quelled the creation of the following gem by eighth grader Lauren, excerpted here:

Uncle Ike is very dear.
Uncle Ike does lots of talking.
He's full of words I shouldn't hear,
and what he says is very shocking
He's sure to give you his opinion
whenever family gets together,
on money politics or religion.
We wish he'd stick to health and weather.

I once outlined the Shakespearean sonnet form to sixth-grade students (prematurely, I'll admit) and asked them to try writing poems in its precise rhyme pattern. The results were unimpressive, but nothing fosters appreciation so much as the firsthand knowledge of its difficulty. Try limericks— they're lots of fun, and frankly, I think a whole new generation needs to discover Edward Lear's *Nonsense Omnibus*.

The Strength of the River, the Voice of Your Eyes

the voice of your eyes is deeper than all roses)
nobody,not even the rain,has such small hands

— E.E. CUMMINGS

I offer up those lines from e.e. cummings mostly because they are exquisitely lovely but also to illustrate how poetry grants us new powers of perception. How can eyes have a voice? What is deep about a rose? How can rain have hands and why would they seem small? Do not underestimate the abilities of your students to appreciate this and give it a try in their own writing. Let them begin by answering questions in their journals: What would the voice of a snowflake sound like? What wisdom does a river possess? Why would roses weep?

Walk away from literal sense and see what songs arise. Nole, a fourth-grade boy, revealed an intuitive sense of metaphor and a profound appreciation of the natural world when he wrote the following words:

> Nothing is quite as strong as the quiet river
> wandering through the land like a snake in the shady grass,
> like a foxtail bristling in the wind.
> Nothing is quite as strong as the quiet.

Ask your students to write a poem of their own that starts out this way, using the adjective and subject of their choice: Nothing is quite as *shy as; soft as; lonely as; brave as*.

An Assortment of Illuminating Activities

Over the years, all good teachers acquire a collection of writing prompts and quick-write triggers that have worked well in their classrooms. Although some of the following are entirely my own, others are borrowed or adapted from the anonymous collective, a shared attic of ideas independently invented or passed around in so many variations as to render their originators unknowable. I am indebted to many fine teachers who have contributed to this communal pool as well as several old dog-eared books, such as *Poetry: Starting from Scratch* by Michael A. Carey and *Rose, where did you get that red?* by Kenneth Koch that are packed with interesting ideas. But these are all just suggestions and starting points. They don't need to be replicated exactly, and it's always a pleasure to come upon a new poem on your own that has possibilities as a writing prompt.

Show Some Emotion

This is a favorite exploratory activity in which students select an abstract emotion and portray it in a tangible way. What color is fear? Boredom? Anger? What would it look like? Taste like? Startling snippets of poetry emerge, and students are well on their way to using metaphor as a writing tool. Here, for example, is Olive's view of envy:

> Envy is someone holding a blue ribbon that you should have won.
> It feels like a small hard tingling in your brain,
> and it covers your eyes with a window of lime green.
> It smells sharp, like gasoline, and pollutes your personal world.
> It is a voice in your head, getting louder and louder.
> It tastes like sweet candy, trying to tempt you.

And here is a fusion of several students' impressions of boredom:

> Boredom is the hum of the television when there's nothing on,
> or the creaking of an old door sliding upon rusty hinges.
> It smells like rain and not being able to go outside.
> It is a square lawn surrounded by a white-washed fence.
> It feels like church taking a long time to get over with.

While we're on the topic of emotions, remember that poetry is a healthy way for adolescents to express the agonies, confusion, and joys of growing up.

List Poems

In his wonderful book, *Poetry from A to Z*, Paul B. Janeczko offers a poetry activity for every letter of the alphabet. Under the letter *L*, for example, he suggests a "list poem" and presents a model called "Things to Do If You Are the Rain" by Bobbi Katz. As you explore poetry on your own you will undoubtedly come upon other possibilities for modeling and inspiration. I am especially fond of "Silver Star" by William Stafford, which begins as follows:

> To be a mountain you have to climb alone
> and accept all that rain and snow. You have to look
> far away when evening comes . . .

These poems open the door for your students to consider what one would do as snow or sky, a basketball or a pencil. Beyond being an exercise in personification or point of view, these might even be metaphors for living one's life. I was surprised at how readily sixth graders took to this exercise. In fact, I can't resist sharing two lovely examples. Kai wrote these instructions on how to be fog:

> Lay low, clinging to a tree
> gently touching a hill.
> Catch the dim sunlight,
> Fill up your stomach,
> eat until you're full,
> then float away
> into the mountains
> and sleep.

Colton chose the wind:

> Make a rustling noise
> Come down the chimney
> Sound like thunder
> Make branches fall down
> Create waves in the ocean
> Rustle trash bags
> Break windows if you dare
> Come when you wish
> Leave when you may
> Be free in the world.

Janeczko suggests a range of serious and humorous topics for list poems, including "things I just can't believe" or "things to do while waiting for your sister to get off the phone." My own students have poetically listed: creative excuses for not doing homework; things they cannot live without; what they learned in the course of the week; what to do on a rainy day; and my favorite, how to have fun. Here is Eduardo's advice on the latter:

> Break a few rules without getting caught.
> Go to the zoo without paying.
> Hit people's doors with your slingshot
> hard enough to scare them but not enough to do damage.
> Explore some places you haven't seen,
> but be careful not to get lost.
> If there is a big pile of dirt,
> hose it down until it turns to mud.
> Roll around and jump in it.

In a workshop I attended led by Naomi Shihab Nye, she suggested asking students to start writing by listing what they'd lost, either sadly gone (a favorite toy), or happily (a bad habit). Her "Yellow Glove" or "Breaking My Favorite Bowl" are wonderful starters for listing and writing about objects lost (and found) or broken. Or begin with the reading of a poem such as William Stafford's "Being a Person," which concludes with these lines:

> How you stand here is important. How you
> listen for the next things to happen. How you breathe.

Ask students to reflect poetically on *what's important.*

Friendship Oaths

These are fun in middle school. Students write elaborate oaths to a chosen friend, describing with tangible images the depth of their feelings, the ways they will uphold their friendship, the things they promise to do together. Remember to steer your fledgling poets from the abstract to the concrete. For example, one sixth-grade boy pledged to his friend that they would "carpool and take each other to Magic Mountain and Knott's Berry Farm" and that someday they would travel in a space ship and see "the planets that float in space and glow in darkness." There is something very touching about these innocent and enthusiastic avowals of love; the decorum of maturity soon renders such feelings silent.

Odes to the Ordinary

In her book *Writing Toward Home*, Georgia Heard offers a collection of "tales and lessons" to stimulate writing. One of them, which she calls "Songs to the Everyday," is an exhilarating way to encourage students to celebrate the ordinary elements of life. A reading of one of Pablo Neruda's fabulous odes to common things (socks, lemons, tomatoes, laziness) may whet the appetite, or a poem such as "The Traveling Onion" by Naomi Shihab Nye. My students enjoyed doing these as short journal entries. Alisa's stomach may have been growling as she wrote this:

> Oh, sandwich! Your bread, turkey, lettuce and salami fill my stomach after it has starved for hours. You are always waiting for me in my backpack waiting to conquer my hunger.

And Austin was thinking longingly of his bed:

> Oh, praise you, mighty and soft bed! You are a big Eskimo that wraps his arms around me and keeps me safe and warm at night.

Colors

For another short exercise, the names of colors are written on strips of paper, and each student selects one at random and writes about the images and feelings the color evokes. One seventh-grade boy described *magenta* as "the color of laughter spilling out of parties like a waterfall." Where do these delights come from? We need to coax them out.

Seeing . . . and Seeing Again

Seven Ways is a writing activity geared to encourage students to see—and see again—looking at the world in a different way each time. The exercise is based on "Thirteen Ways of Looking at a Blackbird" by Wallace Stevens and I thought I invented it but I subsequently encountered a variation in the Kenneth Koch book, *Rose, where did you get that red?* as well as other sources. It doesn't matter who gets the credit; it's a simple but fundamental concept.

You can use the Wallace Stevens poem as a model or start with visions of clouds via the lyrics to Joni Mitchell's song "Both Sides Now"; then challenge students to find at least seven ways of looking at something and craft a poem based on this concept. Megan chose to write about the wind:

> The wind is someone who is willing to play with you.
> It will blow you along the ocean path.
> It brings a tumbleweed to life.
> It blows your hair back with a breeze.
> Wind can touch you, but you can't touch it.
> When a breath of wind comes your way on a hot summer day, you're refreshed.
> The wind is a graceful dance teacher, helping her students, the leaves.

Seashell is a similar activity (origin unknown to me) in which students select a seashell that intrigues them and observe it from all angles, meticulously and holistically, zooming in, and stepping back a bit. What does it resemble with each look? Mariela glimpsed the following:

> First it looks like a Christmas tree.
> Then it turns into a pathway.
> All of a sudden it changes into a big water slide.
> But then I turn around and see a beautiful woman
> dancing in a fancy white dress.
> And finally I see ice cream on an ice cream cone.

While we're talking seashells, George Hillocks developed an activity long ago in which students choose one shell from a large collection and write about it with such precision that someone else could pick it out from all the others based on the description. For more specifics about this activity and insights about teaching writing by an outstanding educator, I recommend George Hillocks' *Observing and Writing* or *Teaching Writing as Reflective Practice*.

Really Knowing

This type of writing starts with a reading of a piece such as Kathleen Norris' beautiful description of rain in her book *Dakota*, a pure rhapsody on the many kinds of rain experienced in South Dakota. She writes:

> Until I moved to western South Dakota, I did not know about rain, that it could come too hard, too soft, too hot, too cold, too early, too late. That there

would be too little at the right time, too much at the wrong time, and vice versa . . . I had not seen the whimsy of wind, rain, and hail; a path in the wheat field as if a drunken giant had stumbled through, leaving footprints here and there. I had not seen hail fall from a clear blue sky. I had not tasted horizontal rain, flung by powerful winds. I had not realized that a long soaking rain in spring or fall, a straight-down falling rain, a gentle, splashing rain is more than a blessing. It's a miracle.

We talk in class about the knowing of something, and how experience creates understanding of a thing in all its true complexity and variation—Eskimos for example, and their thousand names for snow. (A perfect poem to share at this point is "Not Only the Eskimos" by Lisel Mueller.) Students are asked to write about the variations of something they know intimately well: snow, surf, the various moods of morning on a certain street. On the other hand, eleven-year-old Lindsay chose to write about the barn precisely because it was *unchanging*, a place where every morning felt the same, its comforting constancy a refuge from the outside world:

> I walk down the aisle between the stalls to the tack room, where it smells of well-oiled leather and sweat-stained saddle pads. Then I continue on my way to my horse's stall. I duck under the stall guard and stroke her neck. The whole stall is filled with the scent of dirt, horsehair, and wood shavings. I slowly wander into the feed room, where some of the best smells come from, a mixture of sweet and tart scents: sweet coming from the hay and grain, tart from the butte and paddock dry. The barn is my whole world. And that is going to stay that way.

Among my favorite student efforts is a description by a sixth grader named Paco of his mother's walks on the ranch where his family lived and worked. Paco spoke English fluently but still struggled with the written word. I asked him to visualize her walk in all its detail and tell me what he saw. I simply wrote down what he said, and it helped Paco to realize that he had a writer's eye and sensibility. To me it is very pure, perhaps a poem:

> My mother makes good cakes
> and likes to take walks around the ranch.
> She goes up to the yellow bridge.
> She goes to the *huerta*
> where oranges, figs, lemons, and persimmons grow.
> They are juicy and sweet.

She walks to the hacienda.
It is made of adobe like my house in Mexico.
She asks me to come.
It makes her feel better.
Her mind rests from the work.

Students' own rooms or "special places" are tried-and-true topics for sensory descriptive writing and poetry. Spark the spirit with a few readings from literature that convey the essence of a special place, and there are many. One great source is *The Adventures of Huckleberry Finn.* (And this is still my favorite book of all time. Doesn't it bug you that kids think they "know" a book because they've seen a mediocre movie?) Revisit Huck's descriptions of lights flickering from ferry landings, of forays into cornfields and towns to pilfer a watermelon or a chicken, of the way voices carry on the water at night, of lightening storms and river smells and how deep the sky looks as you lie on your back in the moonshine. A classic passage:

> Sometimes we'd have that whole river all to ourselves for the longest time. Yonder was the banks and the islands, across the water; and maybe a spark—which was a candle in a cabin window; and sometimes on the water you could see a spark or two—on a raft or a scow, you know; and maybe you could hear a fiddle or a song coming over from one of them crafts. It's lovely to live on a raft. We had the sky up there, all speckled with stars, and we used to lay on our backs and look up at them, and discuss about whether they was made or only just happened.

If you feel your students might be receptive, bring in a CD and play them a song. I like Kate Wolf's haunting "Red Tail Hawk" with its refrain about the golden, rolling hills of California, but this happens to be about *my* place and I am sure it would not resonate in quite the same way in a different geographical or cultural context. When students write about their rooms, I sometimes play and distribute the lyrics to "In My Room" by the Beach Boys, or "In My Own Little Corner" from Rodgers and Hammerstein's musical *Cinderella*. Be forewarned: these are very un-cool and are sometimes met initially with giggles and theatrical parody. But *you* are creating a special place here: a room where it's safe to play music, indulge in sentiment, express feelings, and share one's writing. You have to stick your neck out a bit if this is going to happen. (I confess: I have even been known to play opera to my sixth-grade students.)

Snapshot Writing

Each student brings in a favorite family photo. What does it evoke? They must zoom in and recall even the memories and details the picture does not readily reveal. (An example by Lenora is included in Chapter 5.)

My Name

This activity is well known among Writing Project participants. A reading of Sandra Cisneros' "My Name" from *The House on Mango Street* is used to inspire a written piece about one's name and identity. (A more recent book, Jerry Spinelli's *Stargirl*, also relates to the idea of renaming and reinventing oneself.) I find that many sixth graders enjoy listening to Johnny Cash singing "A Boy Named Sue" at the start of this writing activity. It, too, touches upon the interesting idea of how one's name helps to shape the life one leads. (And it is astonishing how many kids have never before heard this once hugely popular song, which, by the way, was written by the late poet Shel Silverstein, he so beloved by middle school kids.)

There are various ways to interpret the My Name activity but it consistently yields interesting insights and reflections. A student I knew as Elise, for example, confided that her real name was Elizabeth, but she felt she had not yet grown into that name. Elizabeth, she said, would be:

> classical music played softly in the flickering light of a candle
> a pale lily sitting like a crown atop the waters of a distant lake
> a doe, gracefully leaping through grassy fields and across streams

Time Travel

This is a wonderful way of integrating language arts and social studies. Students write detailed passages about the historical time and place they are studying: an imaginary visit to a marketplace in ancient Babylon, building the Great Wall of China, watching gladiators battle in the Colosseum of ancient Rome. Sensory details are imperative, but grounded in historical knowledge. Clara wrote:

> After crossing the scorched land of desert, this place is the most beautiful I have ever seen. Just yesterday I went to the market in Babylon. There were many people there calling, pushing, and shoving. The most amazing thing happened as the sun was sinking: I saw a sailboat! It was huge, and almost as magnificent as all of

Babylon. The shadows from the setting sun made the mast turn brilliant colors of orange and red. I have sold all my goods and am heading home tomorrow.

The Opulent Possibilities

"It's the words that sing," wrote Pablo Neruda, "they soar and descend . . . They glitter like colored stones, they leap like silver fish, they are foam, thread, metal, dew . . . I run after certain words . . . they are so beautiful that I want to fit them all into my poem . . . I catch them in mid-flight, as they buzz past, I trap them, clean them, peel them, I set myself in front of the dish, they have a crystalline texture to me, vibrant, ivory, vegetable, oily, like fruit, like algae, like agates, like olives . . . And then I stir them, I shake them, I drink them, I gulp them down, I mash them, I garnish them, I let them go. . . .

There will be no questions on the STAR or AP tests that measure how fully your students experience the depth and richness of language, but fluent writers perceive the opulent possibilities contained within the nouns and verbs. Illuminate the room and see what happens. In student poems, I have watched the sky horses who come out at night and glimpsed the glitter of the flower fairies. I have held a fan with a garden of roses in all the colors that roses can be. I have entered a backyard that is a whole world, seen the fog that blocks the path to noon, and learned that the sky is a secret that cannot be told. Some kids have a flair for this and others do not, but every child can be encouraged to scratch out ideas, play with words and phrases, and visit the sanctuary that is poetry. A former colleague, Bruce Brownell, said, "Think of this like building a ship. Lay the keel, attach the ribs, decking, masts, spars, and canvas. Then let the whole thing sail before the wind." And sail we will.

3 Making Words Work
Writing for Results

Language exerts hidden power, like a moon on the high tides.

— RITA MAE BROWN

One of our most important roles as teachers is to help our students acquire a bigger view of the world and a sense of their own presence and power within it. The writing skills that kids acquire in school must eventually translate into real-world communication—problem solving, persuasion, instruction, and explanation. Opportunities are created or lost every day based on the ability to compose an articulate letter, effectively frame an argument, or clearly present a set of facts. This practical and purposeful writing must be clear, concise, and compelling, with no room for error or sloppiness. But few of our students equate the writing they do for an English class with the writing they will do later at work and in the business of life. Our goal is to help them develop the skill and see why it matters.

The Personal Letter

I begin with the personal letter because it simply has no substitute as a direct written connection to another person. I don't care what electronic miracles technology has bestowed upon us—a sincere, articulate letter is a more enduring, effective, and touching means of communicating. Brace yourself for the fact that even in the upper grades many students are unfamiliar with the basic parts and format of a letter; then show them how it's done. Assign letters as homework, check them for perfection, require rewriting, and make sure they are mailed. The thank-you note is a great way to start: it is an art in itself and there is always a reason to send one. Students may begin with words to family or friends, but point them to a wider world as well and urge them to speak up. There is no need to be silent and passive as long as there is a sentiment to express, whether of support or outrage. This means letters to newspaper editors, political representatives, and world leaders. It also means a cheerful note to an elderly lady in an assisted living facility, a thank-you to a writer whose work touched your heart, a suggestion to a local business. Whether or not the recipient responds, completing the act of writing and sending a letter is its own gift.

This letter written by Beth probably made the recipient's day:

Dear Dave:

This fall the students at Dunn Middle School are studying heroes. We've studied superheroes, ancient heroes, American heroes, local heroes, political heroes, and many more. On October 31, our school is celebrating local heroes of the Santa Ynez Valley. I have been thinking about who to invite and then I thought of you. Please come as my guest from 2:00 to 3:00 P.M.

You might wonder why I think you are a hero but it really is obvious to me. When I first moved here four years ago, you were one of the first people I met. Every time I come into the El Rancho market and you are working, I always see you laughing and talking to kids, and not just your customers. Even my friends say they have known you since they were little and thought you were funny and always sweet to kids. You sing, laugh, and tease us like you are our big brother.

Speaking of brothers, both of my brothers worked for you for a long time. They both said that you were a very fair and funny boss.

Thank you for being such a great friend to all the shoppers at the market. Call me if you have any questions at _____. Please let me know if you can come to our festival.

Sincerely,

The Persuasive Essay

Having reached beyond our classroom and made written contact with the outside world through letters, we consider other ways in which the power of language can be used to inform and influence others. One approach is the persuasive essay, which attempts to convince the reader to think or act in a certain way. Of course, in order to convince someone of your opinion, you must first *have* an opinion, so students choose an issue that can be viewed from two distinctly different perspectives, learn a little more about it, and develop a point of view. It isn't hard to come up with such subjects from history, the news, or even Internet listings. I "googled" key words such as "controversial issues for students" and unearthed scores of possibilities. After they select a topic (see the next section Helping Your Students Get Started), remind students to gather ideas and arguments that represent both sides, even if they already have a definite opinion. Trying to understand opposing points of view is a strategy that will always serve them well, and they can present a stronger case if they anticipate the arguments of those who disagree.

The persuasive essay is a fairly traditional assignment, but the following are the section-by-section instructions that I would provide to my students, along with illustrative excerpts from the work of sixth-grade students:

The Introduction

Try to start with a "hook" or attention-getter. It might be a surprising fact, a question, an interesting quote, or an anecdote that will capture the interest of your readers and encourage them to read further. The hook is used to lead readers into the thesis of your essay, which is the opinion or idea that you hope to prove. You should state this opinion clearly right at the start, because it's more important than any other sentence in your essay. It is the reason you are writing—your purpose and challenge. With luck, by the end of the essay you will have proven your thesis and convinced your audience, so present it right away. This beginning section structures your entire essay. Once you have a good introductory paragraph, the rest falls into place more easily.

Here is an example of an opening attention-getter from Nikole's essay about animal experimentation:

> A rabbit's head is locked in place with clamps, and clips keep its eyes open. A scientist drops a drop of oven cleaner into the rabbit's eyes . . . The reward for all this stress caused to the animal is a label saying don't let oven cleaner contact your eyes.

Nikole gets to the point shortly thereafter with a clear statement of her opinion:

> These tests may keep people safer, but it isn't right to harm or kill animals for the advantages of humans.

Proving Your Points

This is the main body of the essay and it should be at least two paragraphs long. Here you will provide further information about the subject and discuss and support your point of view. You will need to go beyond your own knowledge and experience—use the Internet and library, or interview people who are experts on your topic. Build on the facts, examples, and statistics that you gather. Clearly state all your reasons for believing as you do, and don't lose sight of your purpose, which is to persuade the reader that *your* viewpoint is the right one.

Rufus decided to write an essay about whether or not teachers should assign homework. He drew mostly upon his own reflections, but at least he didn't engage in knee-jerk opposition. He argued that homework is actually a good thing when it is designed to help students more clearly understand what was taught in class that day *and* as long as there isn't too much of it. Here is an excerpt of his discussion:

> Homework helps students a lot and prepares you for the work you will have to do out of school because a good life doesn't come on a silver platter. You have to work for it. The teachers want kids to work on what they have learned on their own. That way they can see how much the students understand.

Countering Other Arguments

Try to anticipate the arguments of those who disagree with you and show why their case is weak. Include a paragraph in which you specifically address the points that could be made by those who disagree with you. Then offer evidence that refutes their opinions and shows the strengths of your opinion. This is hard, but it is a valuable strategy.

This excerpt shows how Rufus handled it:

> Lots of people think that homework is robbing kids of their childhood, but the average amount of time spent on homework for a thirteen-year-old is only an hour.

Those who oppose homework are mostly kids. They argue that homework is awful. (I think so too but you can't always get what you want.) They say that homework stresses them out too much. Also it takes away their time outside to exercise and be in nature and it limits the time they spend with their family and friends. Students don't get enough sleep and so they are tired the next day at school. Their case is weak, though, because they are not thinking of the future and how homework will help them.

The Conclusion

Finish with a flourish! Seal the deal! The conclusion summarizes what you have said in your essay, but it is much more than that: it is your final opportunity to convince the reader. Consider ending with a plea for action, a specific suggestion, or a memorable quote. Remember: if you do not convince the reader of your belief, then you have not fulfilled the purpose of the essay.

Nikole, our animal rights advocate, wrapped up her essay with some personal reflection about what she learned from her research. Although I typically discourage reference to oneself and one's feelings about the assignment within the essay, I appreciated her heartfelt search for tangible actions that she could take in her own life. She wrote:

> I learned a lot from the topic I chose. It changed a lot inside me. I've always been against animal testing, but this made me think a lot. Now I'll only buy a shampoo that says not tested on animals on the back. Maybe someday I could make a speech about animal testing and how sick it can get. I had an idea that when a dog or cat at a pound has to be put down maybe they should give it to a lab, and if labs only took dogs and cats from the pounds, maybe that could decrease the number of deaths of dogs and cats. Then dogs and cats that are being put down could at least be useful in medical research. Even though I thought of that idea I still have reservations about animal testing.

Rufus concluded:

> A little homework is good for you, but just enough to understand clearly. I oppose the kind that you get just for work but it doesn't help you. That's why kids have to do homework: to understand more about what the teacher says in class and work on it. So get out there and do your homework.

And Katie, who wrote about saving the wild mustangs of the West, listed some suggestions and concluded with this poetic vision on the next page.

The wind blows through the silky hair of the wild horses as they lope across the horizon, and the sky is painted with splotches of pink, orange and blue. Imagine running in the field of green with your closest friends in the background. My dream is to see this picture that I described. Someday I hope I will.

Helping Your Students Get Started

The success of the persuasive writing assignment has a lot to do with the topics your students select. As I mentioned earlier, there are numerous Internet sites that list controversial issues and provide links to more information. These encompass topics as diverse and complex as capital punishment, prayer in school, gay marriage, gun control, environmental protection, affirmative action, immigration, and animal rights, to mention but a few. Such an abundance of possibilities might seem overwhelming to your students, particularly when they aren't sure what most of these topics really mean; be prepared to guide them to something manageable and age appropriate. A good technique is to ask them to zero in on four or five possible topics about which they can answer "yes" to the following questions:

1. Do I have some idea of what this topic means?
2. Is it interesting to me?
3. Do I care about it?
4. Is it something about which I am curious and would like to learn more?
5. Is it something that people debate and argue about?
6. Can I frame this topic as a question?
7. Is there enough information available to help me understand it and form an opinion about it?
8. Is it substantial enough to write a full essay about it?

It may still take some conferring and compromise to further narrow down the possibilities to one final choice. I like to sell this to kids as a chance to go outside their comfort zone and explore something challenging and thought-provoking. It's true that if a topic is too complex and sophisticated, it can turn into an ordeal, but an easy one like school uniforms or homework can end up feeling flimsy or formulaic. Last year I had a student named

Joe who wanted to write about whether there should be a new episode of *Star Wars*. I appreciated his interest and understood that *Star Wars* aficionados had strong opinions about this, but when Joe started to sketch out ideas he found that he couldn't really develop them into a purposeful essay. The film had already been released, so it seemed like a moot point, and I really didn't want a movie review. Joe abandoned *Star Wars* and bravely shifted to physician-assisted suicide, a term he had been hearing on the news and was vaguely curious about. He ended up writing a compassionate essay in which he declared that it was a "moral crime" to withhold a means of quick death from someone terminally ill and in great pain. He had taken on a tough issue, pondered it sincerely, and even had the courage to articulate a position that conflicted with the official doctrine of his church. Joe's exploration of a difficult subject had encouraged empathy and independent thought.

Please note that this particular assignment is *not* primarily about research skills; it is about thinking and writing. Of course your students will have to do some background reading about the subject in order to understand it, form a viewpoint, and glean facts with which to strengthen that view, but this is essentially an inquiry, not an in-depth research paper. I generally give my students a few tips about how to identify more objective educational websites, sometimes I hand them articles myself or refer them to specific sites that might be helpful, and that's about it. Reading a few factual summaries and overviews are sufficient for our purposes here, as long as two sides are presented. (My students do a more formal and in-depth research project separately as part of our social studies program.)

Finding That Hook

As any reader knows, the first sentence of a story is what immediately draws you in or turns you off. Since we are talking here about a short essay whose purpose is to quickly persuade readers and motivate action, a powerful opening is particularly important. In order to help your students with this element, I suggest you first share a few samples of attention-grabbing opening lines from newspaper editorials, essays, or novels, then send kids on a quest to find some good examples of their own. Point out types of hooks that seem to appear frequently and ask your students to fish around in the notes they have compiled on their issue for any of the following: an image or incident with emotional or shock impact; a challenging question; a revealing quote; a flashback or a prediction about the future; a dramatic fact or statistic; or even a description of a scene. Therein may lie a hook.

Helping Your Students with Revision

Explain to your students that the primary goal of revision is to ensure that the writer's intended idea is communicated clearly to the reader. It's much more fundamental than simple editing adjustments such as spelling and punctuation corrections. As the word suggests, revision implies revisiting and re-visualizing; in the course of revision, the very shape of an essay might change. Kids are loath to do this, and it's easy to understand why. They thought they were pretty much done with the thing and you're asking them to go back in. But rather than relying entirely on you for suggestions, they should learn to examine their own work even before they submit it, answering the following questions and tweaking accordingly:

Self-Review: Meaning
What is my message?
Have I stated it clearly?
Have I supported it with facts, examples, and anecdotes?
Do I need to add more to make it stronger?
Do I need to take something out to make it stronger?
Is my work organized in a logical, purposeful way?

Self-Review: Style
Can I combine any short, choppy sentences?
Do I use certain words repeatedly?
Do many of my sentences start with the same word?
Can I replace these overused words with appropriate synonyms?

Peer feedback is also a helpful tool in revision and a good management technique for teachers with large classes. Middle school students may not be the best editors, but they are certainly qualified to read or listen to another student's piece and determine whether it makes sense to them and holds their interest. The focus will vary depending on the type of assignment, but for a persuasive essay, students should answer the following questions (in writing) about the work of their peers, taking turns as partners or in groups of three or four:

Peer Review: Meaning

Am I able to restate the writer's opinion or main idea?

Are there any portions that seemed confusing to me?

Is the discussion lined up logically and clearly? Can I see a pattern in the way it is organized? Are there any missing pieces?

Can I recall and jot down any of the examples and facts that the writer used to support his or her ideas?

Peer Review: Style

Do the sentences seem to flow smoothly when the essay is read aloud?

Are any particular words or sentence beginnings used repeatedly?

Does the writer seem to care about the topic? Can I sense a "real person" in this writing?

Peer Review: General Feedback

Did the essay capture and hold my interest?

What are the strengths of this essay?

Peer feedback may be done with a preliminary draft or with the "final" draft that the student turns in to you. It isn't easy, either: it demands that kids be thoughtful and attentive, and some will provide more meaningful suggestions than others, but it's useful training for everyone. The next step, of course, is for the writer to actually *read* this feedback, consider it, and accommodate valid comments with appropriate changes. When I "invite the rewrite" I require that my comments (and any peer feedback sheets) will be attached to the revised and corrected final draft. That way I can ascertain whether the comments were at least read and taken into consideration. It drives me crazy when thoughtful and time-consuming feedback is completely ignored.

Why This Matters

The ability to clearly articulate an issue, express an opinion based on facts, and persuade a reader to see it your way has value that is self-evident. There are other benefits less salient but equally profound. Consider Heather, a sixth-grade girl who chose the topic of abortion for this assignment. I thought it was a rather sensitive issue for a sixth grader and told her gently that it was fine if she wanted to do something else. "No, I want to write about this," she explained, "because I believe so strongly that it's wrong. My father was adopted. If his mother had gotten an abortion, he would have never been born." I have seldom seen a student approach a topic with such intensity. She read with furrowed brow, printing out information, writing up notes—and clearly struggling. What troubled Heather was her newfound knowledge that making abortion illegal did not necessarily prevent women from choosing this option but instead forced them into riskier situations. Her essay amazed me. She confessed that in her heart she still didn't feel that abortion was right and maybe there are things like that—things you just *know* or *think you know* for reasons that are emotional or religious and cannot be argued. At the same time, she also discovered that she had compassion for others who might feel differently, and she wasn't sure it was right to subject them to her beliefs. Still, she wondered: if something *is* wrong, isn't it *always* wrong? Heather's final conclusion was not an opinion about abortion at all. It was more or less a statement about the way the world works: Things are not black and white. They are much more complicated than that, and before you make a decision, there's a lot to learn and understand. If that isn't a life lesson, I don't know what is.

A Technical Writing Unit

Middle school students who have been given ample opportunities to develop their expository writing skills are at a great advantage when they enter high school, where the well-written essay continues to be the standard by which a student's command of the language is measured. However, at both middle and upper school levels, it is often frustrating and difficult to get students to revise academic writing with any enthusiasm or true sense of purpose beyond a passing grade. For tips on how to approach this, I spoke to veteran teacher Vickie Gill, who has experimented with various activities designed to motivate students to work and rework their writing until it's right—not because of the threat of a failing grade but because the ultimate goal is to control the accuracy and flow of the writing to produce a product that works. Vickie sequenced the most effective of these activities into a Technical Writing unit that brings a sense of real-world writing into the classroom. (She refers to it as technical writing mostly because it sounds cool, but also because the students have no trouble recognizing the need for precision in these assignments.) Vickie works with high school students, but these activities can easily be adapted to middle school as well.

On-the-Job Writing

After asking her students to scan a long list of jobs and circle the ones that sound interesting as future careers, Vickie makes several posters on which she groups the students with others who have similar goals. These posters are displayed right above the whiteboard at the front of the room so that she can refer to them as she teaches. Here is the complete list of career interests named by Vickie's most recent students:

Politics	Psychiatry or Psychology
Engineering	Peace Corps Service
Photography	Military Service
Banking and Finance	Bartending
Interior Design	Fashion Design
Computers	Commercial Art
Public Relations	Animal Training
Music	Teaching
Medicine or Surgery	Child Care
Journalism	Law Enforcement
Editing and Publishing	Linguistics
Writing	Physical Therapy
Marine Biology	

Next, Vickie challenges the students to locate someone who works in the career they have chosen for themselves and request an on-the-job writing sample to share with the class. Before they can begin, students have to consider the following questions:

1. How will you find this person? Who can help you?
2. How will you contact this person? Email, phone call, letter?
3. How will you compose your request?
4. How will you present this information to the class?

The majority of students become very excited about this project, especially when they actually receive a writing sample. For many, it's the first time they've ever connected writing with a job, a goal, or a real-world activity. Of course many students will not have a clue about what they want to do later in life. In this case Vickie meets with them one-on-one and wheedles a "dream" job out of them. (Middle school kids, who still have at least one foot in childhood, are likely to be even more receptive than high school students to imagining a fantasy job.) Vickie urges her students to think all the way back to kindergarten if necessary: "What did you say when someone asked, 'What do you want to be when you grow up'?" Slowly, hesitantly, the student will respond, "Well, when I was little I wanted to be a race car driver," then shrug it off as if to show that such dreams are stupid. With a kid like that, Vickie does everything humanly possible to help locate someone who knows how to contact a race car driver. After many years of working with students on this project, she observes that the only students who failed to obtain a piece of on-the-job writing have been those who did not follow through on the assignment.

Now that she's helped the kids see that "writing happens" in the real world, Vickie begins a unit on the power of the written word. She shares with her classes the directive she was given years ago by several CEOs who responded to her question, "What should I teach my students that will prepare them to work for your company after they graduate?" These men and women who were in charge of huge corporations knew exactly what they wanted. They urged her to teach kids:

how to work cooperatively with others to solve problems;
how to communicate clearly in writing and speaking;

how to follow directions;

how to learn; and

a work ethic!

Vickie took this advice to heart; she conducts her English classes throughout the year in a manner designed to address these goals.

Assume Nothing

"Speak properly and in as few words as you can," wrote William Penn, "but always plainly, because the end of speech is not ostentation but to be understood." With this philosophy in mind, Vickie begins by focusing on accuracy in writing, a no-frills approach where utility and clarity reign supreme. Here's where brevity *does* have a place. The unit addresses each of the previous CEO directives.

First, Vickie asks students to take out a clean sheet of notebook paper and wait for instructions before they write anything on it. She points to a button she wears that says, "Assume Nothing," letting the kids know that this will be their mantra for the next few weeks. She tells them that she has drawn a random shape on a notebook-sized paper and has listed five specific steps that, if followed exactly, will produce that same shape. They will not be able to see the shape she has drawn until they have completed the five steps. But if they follow Vickie's directions exactly, they should be able to re-create her drawing, which is hidden in the folder. Here are sample instructions:

1. Draw a circle in the center of the page. (About 95 percent of the time, students will passively draw a circle without asking about the exact size. Occasionally someone bravely asks, "How big?" but then accepts a vague answer such as "small.")
2. Draw a line from the left side of the circle to the left edge of the page. (Rarely will student questions pinpoint whether the line is straight or wavy, whether it goes off the edge of the page or stops.)
3. Draw an arrow from the top of the circle to the top of the paper. (Often Vickie will draw her shape with the paper positioned sideways, but the students will assume that she wanted them to hold their paper in the normal alignment for writing.)
4. Draw an X through the circle.
5. Write the letter *A* in the upper right-hand corner of the paper.

When the five steps are finished, Vickie dramatically scans the room and says, "If we were on a job, I'd fire every one of you," and then reveals her own, very different drawing. She teases the students, calling them "rank amateurs," but promises that they will be seasoned professionals when they attempt this again at the end of the unit—and it's true. After a few weeks of trying to follow and write clear instructions, students will not let her move on from step one until she has told them that the circle is the size of the opening on the ball-point pen cap she is holding in her hand. The kids enjoy this activity, and it sets the tone for the importance of accuracy in the assignments to follow.

The first homework assignment requires the students to draw an accurate sketch of their bedrooms. This must be done to scale, and classmates challenge the accuracy of the drawing as the student verbally walks his/her group through the room. Next is an assignment that is done in class, usually while Vickie is working with another group. Over the years, she has collected blueprints of houses that are published in the homes section of the newspaper. She has cut out the floor plans, each of which includes a sketch of the finished house, and put them in numbered clear plastic folders with a black sheet as backing. (I did a Web search using key words such as "home floor plans samples" that turned up thousands of such diagrams; these could easily be printed out for teacher use.)

Vickie chooses houses that are very similar in design so the students must describe the house with such precision that one cannot be mixed up with another. She turns the plastic folders over and spreads them out on the table so the floor plans cannot be seen. Each student takes a floor plan without looking at it ahead of time and hides it in a notebook. Students then find a private corner or table that will allow them to study the floor plan without anyone else in their group seeing which one they've chosen. Their job is to "walk" the group through the house by writing clear and accurate instructions: "When you enter the front door, you will see a living room on the left and a closet on the right. Turn left into the living room, then turn right to face the back of the house. On your right you'll see a fireplace, on your left you'll see a sliding glass door leading out to a patio."

When they've finished writing their instructions, they bring the floor plan back to Vickie's desk and hide it in the folder with the other house plans.

She warns them not to tell anyone anything about the house they've chosen, and to be sure that they haven't written the number of the house anywhere on their directions. The next time their group meets, they spread out all thirty-five house plans on the table and everyone grabs four or five to study while the first person reads her description. As they eliminate houses ("this is a two-story, not a one-story house" or "the kitchen is to the left of the bedroom, not to the right") everyone gathers around the remaining two or three floor plans to discover the exact house the writer is describing. This is actually quite challenging and demands simplicity and accuracy—one wrong turn will throw the whole thing off. If the reader discovers a problem, Vickie has her make notes in the margin and revise the instructions for homework. It takes awhile to listen to a student's description and locate his house; only two or three a day are completed.

Legos

Vickie's next activity requires the same attention to detail, as well as the ability to work cooperatively with others, to produce a piece of writing that can be understood by readers without additional input from the writers. She adapted this idea from a task that was required of students who were competing in a series of challenges called *The Olympics of the Mind*. She purchases a box of Legos and divides the pieces into several matching sets—for example, she will put twenty to thirty pieces in one plastic bag and duplicates of those twenty to thirty pieces in another bag; it's very important that the sets are identical and labeled: *Team 1/Set A*; *Team 1/Set B*; *Team 2/Set A*; *Team 2/Set B*; and so on. Then she randomly divides the students into teams. The activity proceeds as follows:

Day One

Team 1/Set A will find a hiding place where they can create a Lego shape with eight to ten pieces and write step-by-step instructions on how to build the shape (sometimes students can create a screen with a small bookcase on a desk, sometimes Vickie will send students to a neighboring classroom that isn't being used that period to create their shape—the important thing is that the students in the second group cannot see what the first group is doing). The students have thirty minutes to work together to build a shape and then to write instructions so the other team can duplicate the shape without using sketches or drawings of any kind—only words. (This is much harder than it sounds, and the results can be quite amusing.) Next, the team hides the shape in a box along with the directions.

Day Two

When they gather together the next day, Vickie tells the Team 1/Set A group that they are the owners of a large company that makes circuit boards for computers. They have written the instructions for building the circuit boards, which they will now hand to their employees. As a reward for their hard work, they jet off to the Bahamas, where they take a well-earned vacation—without phones, faxes, or carrier pigeons. They will be absolutely unreachable, and the instructions must stand on their own.

The instructions and the Team 2/Set A bag of Lego pieces are now handed to the other team, who work together to translate the directions and re-create the shape. The first team has to sit there and watch, but they cannot groan, moan, oops, or make a sound regardless of what happens. Vickie tells the students she is grading them on their ability to write and follow instructions as well as their participation as a member of a team. Whether or not the second team was able to re-create the shape, they offer the first team feedback as to what was helpful about their written instructions and what was confusing. The first team then revises the instructions if necessary.

Day Three

The second team takes on the challenge of building a shape and creating instructions, and the first team tries to construct the shape.

How-to Manuals

Vickie introduces this activity by telling the sad story of a young secretary who was given the task of writing step-by-step directions for teachers who were about to use a new computerized grading program. She made an error of one single letter, instructing teachers to save to file B rather than the correct file, A. This one-letter mistake had calamitous results: all the grades were lost, the entire system crashed, and the secretary was fired.

The students get the point. This leads into the long-term assignment that requires them to write how-to manuals on a relatively simple task of their choosing. Vickie informs them that she is from another planet (they have no doubt of this already), and she has never seen, for example, a toothbrush—hasn't a clue to how to use it, either. The students may use pictures, drawings, charts, or whatever they want to create these manuals. The manuals must be typed and formatted like a booklet. A few of them are tried in class, and the students know Vickie will do exactly what they tell her to do, so they spend a great deal of time road testing before they present them to the class. (Their idea must be approved beforehand to ensure that they do not pick something too easy or too hard—How to Change a Tire on a Car is too hard; How to Sharpen a Pencil in an Electric Pencil Sharpener is too easy.)

The students are allowed to work in pairs, and they are responsible for bringing all the materials to class on the day their manual is to be tested. Vickie has many funny stories of past disasters, and the kids enjoy writing something that is concise, accurate, and foolproof. (Obviously, students can download directions from the Internet, but because they keep individual writing portfolios, it is quite easy to spot professional instructions.) When possible, Vickie invites the principal or another adult with a sense of humor to come in to test the manuals. The unit is fun and challenging. Interestingly, the best instructions and manuals are often those produced by students who struggle the most with the language, because the real assets in this type of writing are simplicity and conciseness. One of our all-time favorite student efforts—How to Make and Shoot a Spitwad, by Andy—can be seen in Figure 3–1.

The Well-Written Business Letter

We've already considered the importance of letters in a personal, informal sense, but the *business* letter is one of the most powerful forms of writing I know. Many times in my life, a simple business letter has helped me to solve problems and create opportunities. Vickie offers her students an intriguing introduction to this important skill as well. She starts with a pretest that requires the students to draft a three-sentence letter requesting information for a trip. It is rare for a student to write a perfect letter on the first try. Even the best writers will forget the date, the colon after the greeting, or some other small but essential detail. She tells the students to bring their letters to her as soon as they are finished, and she quickly circles writing errors or missing information. At least one student in each class will include far more information than is required to solve the problem.

How to make and shoot a spitwad

(1) Pen (Bic round stic, fine) that the center of it is a white cylinder about the diameter of a cigarette

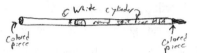

(1) sheet of any binder paper

Take the pen and remove both ends by biting down or wedging the blade of a knife in the grove between white and colored piece in the appropriate place (see diagram below)

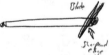

If using blade read step #2a and skip step 2b
If you are using the biting skip step 2a and go to 2b

2a) While holding knife with sharpened edge of blade in the middle of the sharpened part of blade. In grove of white cylinder and colored piece, hold pen tightly with left hand approximately 1 and a half inches away from the side of the pen with blade in it. Hold knife in right hand like you are about to whittle something, pry piece off of pen by pushing blade down into pen and pulling in the opposite direction of white cylinder. YOU ARE NOT SAWING IT BLADE DOES NOT MOVE ALONG PEN (you may have to do this step more than once in order to remove the piece). Then repeat on the other colored piece so you are able to see through the center of the white cylinder like a telescope. see diagram below

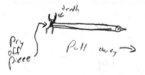

2b) Hold pen with both hands so there is only about an inch off of the first end you wish to remove. Using any teeth you wish (most prefer molars) bite down ONLY ON THE COLORED PIECE TO BE REMOVED(so the pen looks like the diagram below). With both hands hold the rest of the pen tightly and pull away from your teeth in the direction

Figure 3–1a

the pen is pointing. Once that is done repeat on the other end so you can look through the cylinder like a telescope.

Now your pen should look like this…

Once you have accomplished that you are ready to make the projectile to be shot through your pen (like the barrel of a gun)

Take your sheet of paper and rip off a piece about a ¾ inch by ¾ inch square and put in mouth

Begin to saturate with spit and chew like a piece of gum (moving piece around in mouth while chewing and swishing). Once the piece of paper in your mouth is feeling like it is a wet mess that is about to come apart in your mouth, it is ready

Using your mouth muscles move paper to he tip of your tongue and with lips hold it there.

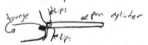

Put one end of the white cylinder up to the center of your lips directly on top of the ball of paper and spit and using tongue push the paper into the cylinder

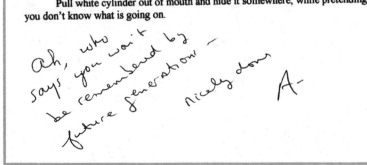

Without removing cylinder from mouth, adjust it so you are able to blow through it strait (so its not to the side or aimed up or down) DO NOT BREATH THROUGH TUBE UNTIL READY. Move your tongue out of the way and aim as best you can at your target, when prepared blow a hard fast quick burst of air through tube launching spitwad through the air.

Pull white cylinder out of mouth and hide it somewhere, while pretending that you don't know what is going on.

Ah, who says' you won't be remembered by future generations — nicely done A-

Figure 3–1b

After she has scanned each letter, Vickie shows the students the specific format she will require for the remainder of the unit. (She uses modified block because most of the letters will be short and it uses up some of the white space on the page; it also forces the students to follow directions and pay attention to details.) She then suggests a few real-life situations that require the students to either solve a problem or create an opportunity in a concise yet persuasive manner. The situations may involve a request for information about an activity, product, or place; a letter to a mentor asking for advice; questions regarding a scholarship; a suggestion to a city council about setting aside an area for skateboarding; a community service idea; a work proposal; a cover letter for submission of one's writing for publication; and perhaps an inquiry on arranging to meet with one's congressional representative during a trip to Washington, D.C.

Before tackling their "real-life" letters, the students write practice letters using imaginary scenarios such as the four that follow:

Problem Solving with the Business Letter

Choose one of the following scenarios and write the perfect letter.

Problem 1: You purchased a used car from Bubba's Motors, a local Chevy dealer. The air conditioner has never worked properly. You've taken it back several times, but this problem is never really fixed—the car tends to overheat when the air conditioner is on, especially when going uphill. Write a letter to the regional manager explaining the problem and offering a possible solution.

Problem 2: You are interested in attending Emerson College after you graduate. Write a letter requesting an application and information on financial aid.

Problem 3: You and your spouse have separated, but you have a number of credit cards in both your names. Write a letter to one company asking them to cancel your joint account and issue a new card in your name only.

Problem 4: Yesterday you introduced yourself to Holly Delaney, who runs a hip surf shop in your town. It turns out she is hiring kids to work there in the summer—not only does this match your skills and interests, but the hours are ideal and you've heard that she is a great boss. Write a letter to Holly telling her how much you enjoyed meeting her and expressing your interest in job possibilities for the summer.

This is a very manageable activity because the typed letters are short and to the point. Vickie works with her students in groups so she can quickly circle errors and request revisions. It's a good opportunity for individualized mini–grammar lessons, for it allows her to review the concepts of usage within the context of the individual student's syntax and diction, a far more useful format than having the entire class complete the same worksheets. This is one of the few times Vickie requires absolute perfection in her students' writing; she awards a "100" for a perfect letter and reduces the grade by ten points for every revision. The process emphasizes that careful proofreading is important, and even the most reluctant writer can see why an inquiry about a scholarship or a business letter requesting a job application would have to be as perfect as possible. Each revision is stapled to the final copy and placed in the student's writing portfolio, an excellent way to trace a student's progress—and the student is competing with herself rather than with the rest of the class. This is the unusual situation in which writing *too much* can be a detriment and a student who struggles with the written word can excel.

Brandon wrote *his* practice letter to a Mr. Hatch of Bubba's Motors in response to the hypothetical problem of the malfunctioning air conditioner. He went through three revisions, tending to incorrect spacing and punctuation, correcting typographical errors, and clipping a redundant phrase here and there, and produced this succinct and effective final version:

Dear Mr. Hatch:
I have recently purchased a used car from your lot at Bubba's motors. The air conditioning does not work properly; it overheats when going up hill. As a result, I have brought it into the shop many times, but it still continues to malfunction. If it is not too much to ask, I'd appreciate the proper treatment or even a new air conditioner. Thank you for your time.
    Sincerely,

Next, students write their real letters to real people, and these final letters are mailed. Most kids love to receive mail, and it is exciting when responses come in. At the high school level, it is easy to see how a letter to a college helps the students make the connection to the utility of writing and starts them thinking more clearly about what they need to accomplish in the next few years to reach their goals. But even at the middle school level, sending out business-type letters that trigger concrete action can clarify the link between writing and setting things right, or bringing a dream closer to reality. Students are empowered by the realization that they can indeed reach the world outside with their words.

When they are comfortable with the format, Vickie encourages her students to write business letters that have nothing to do with their class assignments. They send letters to newspapers, magazines, and community leaders who can help them change things. She knew she was on the right track with this unit when one of the biggest troublemakers in the school burst into her room during lunch. He claimed that he'd been wrongly accused of some act of vandalism and was extremely angry with the vice-principal. In the past, his fury usually played out in some kind of destructive action, but now he just wanted to use a computer. He immediately accessed the word-processing program and began to pound out a well-written business letter to the principal, the school board, and the local newspaper. He truly understood that the written word could be as powerful as his fists, and he was using something he'd learned in his English class to solve a problem and perhaps even create an opportunity. His teacher was proud.

Working in Groups with a Larger Class

Vickie does everything in her power to work with her students in small groups. For starters, she has ten computers in her classroom. She obtained computers over the years by writing proposals submitted to the school board, but in her current job at a private school her students use computers donated by parents who have upgraded to something more powerful. Depending on the size of the class and the room, she can divide the kids into two or three groups: One group works with her, one group works on the computers, and one group works on assignments at their seats. She rotates the groups approximately every twenty-five minutes. She has taught this unit with as few as ten students and as many as thirty-three in the same room. Sometimes she'll teach two or three different units to two or three groups—perhaps poetry, literature, and technical writing—based on the needs and interests of her students. At other times she'll teach the same unit to the entire class and divide the students into four or five groups, which allows her to move about the room in the role of a facilitator as the students work through the activities.

A Sense of Purpose

John Gregory Dunne once observed that writing is just "a manual labor of the mind, a job, like laying a pipe." Perhaps it's true. Yet nothing is as exhilarating as writing that gets the job done, or as self-reinforcing as the tangible results it can yield. The overriding idea here is that *words work*, and writing activities are more meaningful to students when they encompass a concrete sense of purpose and a visible connection to the real world.

4 Book-Based Journeys
Writing About Literature

I n literature we lose ourselves in lives not our own, assimilating new experiences, connecting these to what we know, and expanding our vision of what is humanly possible or imaginable. How do we acknowledge and encourage this miraculous potential in the middle school classroom? Remember first that reading is its own reward, and that not every book needs to generate a writing assignment. Give students ample opportunities to read solely for pleasure and to experience a book in its own way. "Leaving a child alone to savor a book," writes Susan Ohanian, "to get from it what he or she will, and then holding your tongue when the child closes the book, requires a tremendous act of faith—faith in children and faith in books." So, for starters, have some faith.

That said, there is still no better springboard for writing than reading, for it so broadens the scope of the world from which your students speak. Conversely, reading becomes more meaningful when writing occurs: writing about literature is a way of experiencing it more fully, responding to it, interacting with it, and extending it, and this doesn't usually happen by itself. The key is to create assignments that elicit genuine thought and creativity rather than simple recall of facts or plot structure. Maybe that's so obvious it didn't need to be said, but such assignments demand imagination and effort and are not often found in prepackaged literature-unit workbooks. To borrow the term used by Robert Probst, a professor of English education at Georgia State University, literature is an *invitation*. He writes:

> The books, and stories, and poems we lay before our students are not, after all, simply instruction manuals or repositories of information. They are instead invitations to a passionate engagement with human experience.

All readers are implicitly invited to ask questions and analyze, to enter into a conversation about the fundamental issues of life, and to tell their *own* stories. Your job is to render such invitations explicit. Think not in terms of skills but of big picture ways to engage the whole child in the wake of a book.

Choosing Books

We'll get into some specific ideas for integrating writing and literature in a minute. First, I want to introduce you to my colleague Linda Smith, a veteran teacher, middle school director, and true aficionado of young adult fiction. I asked Linda for her thoughts when I began writing this chapter. Here is an excerpt of her initial email response:

> I hold fast to my belief that great literature does not mean college-level reading for middle school kids. I do inspire kids to take intellectual leaps with some of the books we choose, but I prefer highly engaging age-appropriate books that make kids think. It is that thinking process that allows them the ability to truly understand what a thesis is, what a plot is, how characters develop, and how they might apply these concepts to their own writing and their own lives.

A list of fifty outstanding middle school books—from perennial classics to relative newcomers—is included at the end of this chapter. There is nothing scientific about this list: I simply asked colleagues (and kids) to name their favorite books for young adults and threw in a few of my own as well. You may find a few quirky ones that represent individual taste, but those titles followed by an asterisk were mentioned numerous times. The resulting assortment includes books that appeal to a variety of tastes and a range of abilities. Some are excellent books for classroom discussion and writing, while others would be best suited for individual choice reading, and if the book is part of a series, I only mentioned one title in the series. Naturally this list is just the tip of a very large iceberg, but there are some terrific suggestions here.

For recommendations about brand-new young adult literature, one excellent source is the website of the Young Adult Library Services Association (YALSA), which compiles an annual list of the Best Books for Young Adults. (Go to www.ala.org/ala/yalsa.) Another exceptional website, nancykeane.com, offers All Together Now (ATN) book lists with hundreds of suggestions that are categorized by theme (such as gossip, peace, rejection), school subjects, grade level, similarities to known favorites, and many other helpful categories. These reading lists were begun several years ago by Dale Copps as part of a librarian collaborative project. I am always astonished by the wealth of information people have taken the time to gather and present on the Internet. Along with the bad and the ugly, there's an awful lot that's good.

A Few Words About Classroom Reading

There is nothing more delicious than sitting in a comfortable spot all by yourself, lost in a book. In a middle school classroom setting, however, the required "core" books should be at least partly read aloud by the students, punctuated by teacher-led interruptions for guided discussion. I know it's painful at times for both the reader and the listeners but oral reading offers several benefits. It's a good opportunity for teachers to ask leading questions; highlight vocabulary words, allusions, and complexities that would have otherwise gone unclarified and ignored; and ensure that the exploration of these particular books is a shared experience. (Furthermore, it's amazing how many reading problems and learning issues can be detected when a student reads out loud.) I decided to abandon this practice for a while in response to the pleas of some of my most avid and sophisticated student readers; I reinstated it after I discovered that much was lost. Silent reading by students of their individually chosen books still has its honored place, of course, and it's fun to hear what books kids love and recommend. But the books we assign in our classroom are not necessarily the ones students would choose on their own, and kids often need some assistance in appreciating and understanding them.

I usually read the first chapter out loud to the class and I do so with all the dramatic expression it demands. Thereafter, we do what teachers call "popcorn reading" in which kids read a few paragraphs and then randomly call someone else's name to take over. Here are a few examples of the kinds of questions to ask as the reading proceeds:

What does this section make you wonder about?
Can you foresee something here that will dramatically shift the plot?
What big decision is the character facing here?
What consequences do you think that decision might have?
Does this remind you of anything else we've read?
Does this remind you of anything in your own life?

Valuable discussion and deeper comprehension ensue, and confusion is aired and cleared up. (Confusion, as Sheridan Blau says, is the beginning of wisdom, and if you point this out to your students they will look at you, confused.) Mind you, we're not beating the book to death here, just making sure we're all more or less on the same page. Assign chapters for homework, of course, with follow-up the next day. Students may respond to some of your discussion questions in their journals and then share these. Talk flows more readily when they've had a chance to think and write first. Another helpful strategy, particularly with larger classes, is to organize students into small teams and dispatch them to discuss particular questions and jot down responses before reconvening for a whole group conversation. Conversation feels easier and less risky in a small group, and students have more confidence expressing their thoughts with the whole class when they have been able to test drive these in a team context first. Kids become the experts on whatever questions their teams discussed and they can take the lead when those topics come up in the whole group.

I've even resorted to gimmicks in order to facilitate engagement. For example, I call it a game and write general conversation starters on strips of paper that students choose randomly. They keep their books at hand for easy reference if needed and may pass the strip to the classmate on either side of them if they cannot think of anything to say, but points accrue for insightful reflections or genuine effort to participate. Examples of starters: "I like this line, and here's why" or "this reminded me of . . ." or "this part confused me because. . . ." Occasionally I've written the prompts on tags in teacups and declared it a tea party. It's silly, but theatrical and fun. I like to think such start-up measures help lure the shy students out of their silence and perhaps mitigate the terror some kids feel about being called on. I cannot overemphasize the value of the conversations that take place in class and the larger thematic issues to which they lead. They may be time-consuming, but they provide the groundwork for meaningful writing.

Ideas for Writing Creatively About Books

The possibilities for writing creatively about books are as wide as your imagination. The following are just a few.

Short Stories

One interesting concept Linda Smith has often used is to ask students to write a short story in the same genre as the book they just read. For example, if they read *Fahrenheit 451*, they will write a science fiction story. Obviously this is an overwhelming assignment if it is left that open-ended, so start by facilitating a brainstorming session to generate possibilities. Be sure to take a look at theme and message as well. For example, *Fahrenheit 451* may well represent an extreme example of being careful what you ask for—the absence of books may sound like a dream to some students—but in reality, it becomes a social nightmare. In the course of such discussion, kids begin to conjure up their own scenarios, plot ideas emerge, and it becomes much easier for them to start writing. Different kids may use the same plot; it is fascinating to see how each one develops the story.

By the way, this is a good opportunity to talk about literary archetypes. It is exciting for students to begin to recognize classic patterns and to develop their own stories along those lines. Linda advocates using familiar movies to introduce archetypes: "It's much easier to describe the reluctant hero, for example, if I demonstrate how it plays out in a movie . . . whether it is *Home Alone, Lord of the Rings*, or a Disney cartoon." Once students have the classic pattern figured out, list essential components that they must include in the plot of their own story, such as a change in the main character from beginning to end, and tests and obstacles he or she must pass or overcome. Again, this is best accomplished after several plots have been discussed with these concepts in mind. (See also the Steal the Plot activity mentioned later.)

Variations on Found Poetry

This activity involves selecting particularly luminous or compelling lines and phrases from a book and arranging them in the form of a poem, weaving in one's own words and connections as desired. It is a well-known idea among language arts teachers. However, there are several different ways to approach it. Linda recommends first assigning specific pages from which to select lines, and a reminder—samples always help. Prepare the kids by helping them understand key elements to look for in a good poem, such as similes, metaphors, alliteration, precise adjectives, and strong verbs. This is a great way to focus on pages that deserve to be reread and it also demonstrates how a poem arrangement can change everything. Georgina harvested a chapter of *The Merry Adventures of Robin Hood* by Howard Pyle and imagined the stroll excerpted here:

Sweet was the greenwood
as she sauntered along the paths.
Hedgerows were green
and flowers bedecked the forever-ending meadows.
She lay down in the soft grass bedding by a cool pond
and drifted soon into a deep, luscious sleep.

And Beth dared to rhyme:

O passed the gentle springtime
More beautiful by the hour
Its silver showers and sunshine
Its meadows and its flower,
Daisies pied and yellow cuckoos sing
The pink primroses a sign of spring
The moist verges of running streams
The tenderness of thyme,
lovelier than my dreams.

Another twist is to have students choose one word on a page and one word from each line after that, up to fifteen words. They then use each word somewhere on one line of their poem, filling in the rest of the line with their own words.

Ask them to write three four-line stanzas; this allows them to throw out three words. Or ask them to select an exceptional line from the book to use as either a first or last line in a poem. (This is a good time to point out the special importance of the first and last lines of the book itself.) Feel free to invent your own formula. This type of activity gives kids an immediate way to access a book through writing and helps them to feel the texture of the language.

Conversation and Dialogue

Another thought-provoking writing activity is to name two characters, each from a different novel, and ask your students to create a dialogue or script that reveals what they would say to one another. You may require that they discuss a particular topic, or just leave it open-ended, but the conversation must reveal some knowledge of the personalities or experiences of the characters. I first heard this suggestion from Tom Romano, and he offered a fascinating example by a high school student who envisioned a meeting between Julius Caesar and Atticus Finch. *The Wizard of Oz* by L. Frank Baum and *Beowulf: A New Telling* by Robert Nye were both on our sixth-grade reading list last year. Here is an excerpt from a rather competitive exchange sixth grader Luke invented between Beowulf and Dorothy:

> BEOWULF: Hey, little girl. Sellin' Girl Scout cookies? I'm not, because I'm rough and tough and I'm gonna kill a monster.
> DOROTHY: Big deal. I killed a wicked witch with only a bucket of water.
> BEOWULF: Oh, yeah? I killed Grendel with my own bare hands.
> DOROTHY: Well, I've been somewhere over the rainbow and you've only been to the disgusting fen.

To stretch this assignment, require that the true voices and personalities of characters be accurately captured. I don't think Luke succeeded, but he did create an amusing tit-for-tat that demonstrated his recall of events.

Choosing a Friend

Upon reading a particular book, students choose a character that would most likely be their friend, and then they write an essay about why they feel they can relate to this character. After we finished *The Outsiders* by S. E. Hinton, for example, Matt chose the character of Johnny to be his special friend. Here is an excerpt of Matt's essay:

> Of all the characters in *The Outsiders* by S. E. Hinton, Johnny Cade would be the friend I choose. I look for many qualities in a friend. For example, a friend should be a caring and sensitive person. If they are not caring and sensitive they will not want to open up to you about their personal problems. A friend should also be fun, loving, and exciting to have around. Johnny is the one character who shows all these traits.
>
> Johnny shows these characteristics this way, he protects Pony Boy when they are in the church hideout. When they needed supplies he went to go get them early in the morning so no one saw Pony Boy. When he got back from the store he got out his knife and cut their hair so nobody would know it was them. Johnny is also a good friend because he got Pony Boy his favorite book that he wanted to read. He enjoys reading like Pony Boy does. This is one of the reasons that he got the book for Pony Boy. He also likes poems that he showed in the book. Johnny is really sensitive. This is because he got jumped by a boy named Bob. Also, he was treated badly by his parents. He shows that he is caring when he let Pony Boy read him the book. He also acted like a brother to Pony Boy when they were hiding out. He is a hero because he saved the kids from the church fire.

Letters to or About Characters

There are various interpretations of the letter-writing assignment, and kids enjoy it because it involves a sort of role-playing on the page. Basically, students *become* a character and write a letter (to another character) about what has happened to them and their feelings about it. (Diary entries in the voice of a character also work, but without the direct connection to another character.)

An interesting variation is to ask students to respond to a request for a letter of recommendation on behalf of a character. I have read many letters, for example, stating reasons why (or why not) Tom Sawyer would fit in well at our middle school, based upon the virtues and flaws he demonstrated in the course of his adventures. After our students read *Robin Hood*, I provided the starting sentence and sixth grader Cyrus wrote the following intriguing letter to our school's director:

> Dear Mrs. Smith,
>
> I understand that Robin Hood of Sherwood Forest has applied for admission to Dunn Middle School, and I have been asked to provide a letter of recommendation.

I have known Robin for one and a half years. I work closely with the Sheriff of Nottingham and have seen Robin's evil activities in that dreadful forest. He has made a mockery of the sheriff and his men.

Unfortunately I do not believe Robin Hood should be allowed to go to Dunn. This would be a mistake on many levels. Your school has clear policies about behavior and I don't think he would be able to comply. Robin Hood may steal to give to the poor, but it is definitely not okay to take someone's lunch money. Carrying sharp weapons like swords and arrows in school is definitely not appropriate. Robin is not especially violent, but he may pull a prank on someone when least expected. For example, you might laugh at his green tights and funny looking hat, and he might just leave a surprise in your lunch.

Robin Hood's lunch bag mostly consists of a large piece of venison that he claims to have killed with his bow when it was not even hunting season. Another content of his lunch is a flask of ale! Surely he will urge fellow students to try. He will not be smart about this.

Considering all the criminal activities above, Robin Hood is definitely not a good candidate for admission to Dunn Middle School. We can't let this juvenile delinquent poison the students of this school. However, I do recommend a 28-day program to treat his drinking and behavior. After such intervention he might become a suitable applicant after all.

Sincerely,

And here is an excerpt from a four-paragraph letter Ellen wrote expressing her candid reservations about Donald Zinkoff, the main character of Jerry Spinelli's book *Loser*:

Academically, Donald has some issues. I think he would need more practice in writing courses because you can't exactly tell what he is trying to say in his writing. He also has some little problems with his spelling and grammar. One time he got an A on an easy spelling test and everybody was teasing him saying you got an A and he was taking it seriously. It was sort of sad how gullible he was. I know that he tried to make friends and I felt sorry for him, but Dunn Middle School has many expectations and I really don't think he can meet them.

Miscellaneous Writing

Sometimes it's fun to honor different types of writing that are often overlooked, such as recipes or travel journals, and these can be readily linked to a book. For example, when the kids in Linda's class were reading books and short stories from World War II, they collected items from home related to that era. These could be as simple as a penny or as fascinating as old recipes and photographs. By the end of the month, the class had created a museum of 1930s and '40s items. Their assignment was simply to write about some aspect of the collection. The results included cookbooks, booklets on fashion or music, and letters about rationing, victory gardens, and other details of day-to-day life on the home front. This kind of immersion into the setting of a novel adds a whole new dimension to the experience of literature.

New Twists and Old Standbys

It's nice to have an assortment of generic ways to spark student responses to literature that can be customized to a particular book. Here are a few— some new and quirky, others tried and true. Ask your students to do any of these or your own variations, but be sure to offer several choices:

- Rewrite the ending, change a scene, or create a sequel.
- Rewrite a chapter specifically from the point of view of another character.
- Write a poem related to the setting, theme, a character, or an event in the book.
- Pretend the book has been made into a movie: write the review and create a poster, too.
- Based upon what you believe to be the qualities of a good novel, develop a literary award and present it for a book you have read. Be sure to explain the criteria for winning this new award and how this book met those criteria.
- Write the headlines and newspaper report of a key scene from a particular novel. In fact, why not create other features for the newspaper as well, such as ads that would pertain to the time and place, a weather report, appropriate sports, or the invented mishap or accomplishment of some secondary character?
- Compare and contrast two novels that you have read this year.
- Compare and contrast two characters from the same or from different books.
- Compare and contrast a character from a book with yourself or someone in your real life.
- Be one character and discuss all the other characters from that perspective.

- Discuss an experience you have had in your own life that is in some way similar to the experience of a character in the book.
- Show how a character changes and develops through the course of the novel.
- What problems did a character encounter? How were these solved?
- Consider and critique the way a character solved problems. Were these the best strategies and solutions? Were there alternatives that might have been more effective? How would these have affected the outcome?
- Write an advice column in which characters from the book ask questions about their problems and you, Dear Abby, respond.
- Write an obituary for a character . . . or a ballad about a character.
- Be the author and discuss what part of the book was the most enjoyable or most challenging to write.
- Consider the view of the world this book leaves you with. Is fate fair? Do people get what they deserve? Does good prevail over evil?
- Steal the plot. Write a story that uses the same basic plot but with different characters and a different setting.

A Few Rules for Writing About Literature

In my middle school mind, I try to focus on nontraditional, literature-based writing assignments that encourage imagination and creativity. Nevertheless, there are certain conventions to writing about literature, and students should know these things. Here are some basic principles to impart to your students:

1. Even though your teacher knows what you are writing about, you need to state the full title and the author of the book as you begin.
2. But *do* come up with a title for your paper that is more than just the title of your book. Your title should give some clue about how you are going to approach this discussion. For example, Ponyboy Curtis: The Outsider Friend I Would Choose.
3. Do not lean too heavily on general adjectives of praise or criticism such as *fantastic, interesting,* or *boring.* That's too easy. Reveal these

opinions in the context of a larger discussion that demonstrates what you mean.

4. Do not speculate without providing evidence. For example, rather than simply saying *why* a character does something, offer specific actions and quotes that demonstrate these motivations or add credence to your idea.

5. When referring to something that happened in the course of the book, it is customary to use the present rather than the past tense. (My students find this baffling.) Although we know the story took place over a century ago, we would write, "Huck fakes his own murder and runs away."

6. Do not confuse the narrator's voice with that of the author. The narrator may be a character whose perspective is completely different from the author's.

Reading Teaches Writing

Proficient writers have one thing in common—they read. Reading is the best way to absorb subtleties of style and technique, to understand character and voice, to "see" how it's done. Just as a painter studies the works of the masters to better understand how truly great art is created, so too, a writer delves appreciatively into literature. Whether or not one consciously explores the backstage *how-to*, a reader over time begins to acquire a sense of what works and what doesn't. As novelist Patricia Duncker says, "Anyone who writes seriously and well is bound to be an impassioned reader because that is how you learn."

This need not be left to chance: *consciously* approaching literature as a writer adds yet another dimension to teaching it. With his AP senior English classes, my colleague Jason Whitney deliberately dons this hat and keeps it on. He asks his students to think of the author as a peer who can show them how to write well. "Ask not *what happened*," he suggests, "but rather ask *how did the writer make it happen*?" Jason likens it to a post-game analysis in which spectators might ponder what decisions of the coach affected the game and its outcome. In the same way, he asks his students to consider what choices a writer made to create an effect, or what techniques were used to convey the overall message of the work: How, for example, does the use of certain metaphors contribute to the general mood of the story? Or, how does the writer present different points of view within the novel?

But there are varying levels of appreciation. A teacher's role in middle school is to help students discover the intentionality and methodology of the writing, yes, but equally important, to awaken them to ways it relates to their own lives and to the world. Even when not accompanied by meticulous analysis of technique, reading teaches writing because it is a never-ending source of inspiration, ideas, and examples. Sixth grader Justin is an ardent reader of complex fantasy tales, and happens to be a terrific writer as well. I can see the influence of the books he has read in his style and themes, but he is also beginning to develop his own unique voice. One of Justin's recent journal entries says it all: "I love reading stories because they leave ideas swimming in my head. I love being sucked into books and watching them as if they were movies, but what I really love is watching my own stories unfold."

The study of literature is not about dissecting a work, but about finding ways to access, experience, and react to it, and writing is a means to achieve this. What a book ultimately means is a combination of what the author wrote and what the reader experiences through the text. The literature-based writing that students do should be designed to foster this exploration, rendering the text real by linking it to their lives and feelings, and encouraging them in their own creative expression.

Middle School Books: Fifty Random Recommendations

The Hitchhiker's Guide to the Galaxy by Douglas Adams

Nothing but the Truth by Avi

Speak by Laurie Halse Anderson

I Know Why the Caged Bird Sings by Maya Angelou

Hope Was Here by Joan Bauer

My Brother Sam Is Dead by James and Chris Collier

Tunes for Bears to Dance To (and other books) by Robert Cormier

*Walk Two Moons** (and other books) by Sharon Creech

Catherine, Called Birdy by Karen Cushman

*A Northern Light** by Jennifer Donnelly

I Know What You Did Last Summer by Lois Duncan

*Ender's Game** by Orson Scott Card

The House of the Scorpion by Nancy Farmer

Bull Run by Paul Fleischman

Summer of My German Soldier by Bette Greene

*The Outsiders** by S. E. Hinton

Downriver by Will Hobbs

The Raging Quiet by Sherryl Jordan

Flowers for Algernon (Charly) by Daniel Keyes

A Wrinkle in Time by Madeleine L'Engle

*To Kill a Mockingbird** by Harper Lee

The Chronicles of Narnia by C. S. Lewis

*The Giver** (and other books) by Lois Lowry

Crooked by Tom and Laura McNeal

Fallen Angels by Walter Dean Myers

Hatchet (and other books) by Gary Paulsen

A Day No Pigs Would Die by Robert Newton Peck

In the Hand of the Goddess (Song of the Lioness) by Tamora Pierce

Imani All Mine by Connie Porter

The Chosen by Chaim Potok

The Golden Compass by Philip Pullman

Angus, Thongs, and Full-Frontal Snogging by Louise Rennison

The Light in the Forest by Conrad Richter

Harry Potter* series by J. K. Rowling

Esperanza Rising by Pam Muñoz Ryan

Holes by Louis Sachar

Lucy the Giant by Sherri L. Smith

A Series of Unfortunate Events by Lemony Snicket

The Witches of Worm by Zilpha Keatley Snyder

Stargirl* (and other books) by Jerry Spinelli

Of Mice and Men by John Steinbeck

The Road to Memphis by Mildred D. Taylor

The Hobbit by J. R. R. Tolkein

The Invisible Thread (In My Own Words) by Yoshiko Uchida

Dicey's Song* (and other books) by Cynthia Voigt

The Color Purple by Alice Walker

101 Ways to Bug Your Teacher by Lee Wardlaw

Dragonwings by Lawrence Yep

Briar Rose by Jane Yolen

The Pigman by Paul Zindel

---

* These books were mentioned numerous times.

5 Bringing Writing to Life
Wisdom and Discovery Through Memoir

If we learn not only to tell our stories but to listen to what our stories tell us
. . . we are doing the work of memory.

— PATRICIA HAMPL

One spring day when he was about ten years old, Robert was playing in the backyard, idly aiming his slingshot at birds but generally expecting to miss. When a jay fell lifeless to the ground, he was stunned. "I didn't have a happy hunter feeling," Robert wrote, describing the incident in a sixth-grade essay, "I felt sad and shattered." Out of all the birds in the world, he told himself, one could not possibly matter very much, but in his heart he knew that he had killed something for no reason at all. "Life is precious," he concluded, "It can be lost in a second, and I had taken it away from a bird. I realize now that life is worth more than anything, and that we should respect things for what they are, not punish them for what they are not. When you mess with death, there is no victory."

The experience of killing the jay obviously affected Robert deeply but he had never described it so completely or understood its larger meaning until he wrote about it. This chapter is about interpreting experience through writing, about unexpected discovery, about life lessons and epiphanies. It is about giving students opportunities to speak and write about their experiences, and showing them how to listen for the lessons in their own words. Welcome to the inner room of memory.

Life Teaches

My interest in this type of writing began with a series of interviews my middle school students and I conducted with various people in our community as part of an ongoing oral history project. There was at least one point in every interview at which the subject would offer a basic lesson or understanding about life. Such lessons were usually preceded by colorfully drawn stories and anecdotes that illustrated the wisdom or explained how it had revealed itself. In some cases, the individual's recollections seemed to shape themselves according to fundamental themes that were woven throughout the narrative.

Throughout *his* interview, a well-known local cowboy used various anecdotes to impress upon kids the importance of being open to unexpected opportunities. He repeatedly pointed out how a seemingly small and random event can dramatically change one's life. As a young boy in Texas, for example, he took on the care of a "bum colt" that had been born at a prosperous nearby ranch. He described the unanticipated outcome:

> About two years later, a guy come by and bought the horse from me. Horses weren't worth much in those days. This horse was two years old, and he offered me $85 for it. No one had heard of a horse bringin' that much money, so I sold him, no questions asked. Well, my brother-in-law couldn't wait to tell the people at the ranch how much I got for the colt! So this colt was responsible for me gettin' a job at this ranch. Little things can sometimes turn into big things. They said, "If he can sell a bum colt for $85, he can come down here where he can work with some good horses." So it's funny how things in life just come around. You don't go out seekin' these things, but when they show up at your front door, you gotta recognize them.

Another of our interview subjects, a beloved teacher at our school, told us the following story about the day she gave birth to her son:

> I got up from my bed and went to look at my son. I went down to where the babies were, and he was in his bed sleeping. It was his first night. His

first night out in the world. The nurse who was with me had just come out from delivering another baby, and she said to me, "My daughter is twenty-one years old today." So her baby was twenty-one. That's a pretty important age. She and I stood next to each other. There were just two babies in there, and I sort of had a feeling of a big circle. Within that circle, there were many pictures—pictures of light and dark, day and night, happy, sad, high, low, birth, death, opposites, and it was—to me, what it said was: This is life. You choose it all. If you're gonna live, you have to say yes to all of it. That was kind of an epiphany. It came from having a child, and the love I felt immediately was so big, so big that you could cry all the time.

And yet another interviewee, a Native American storyteller, described a series of tragic events in his life that helped form his personality and understanding of the world. One such incident was as follows:

I had a sister who died of cirrhosis of the liver. I had realized my mortality as a young boy. I knew I was going to die. But I've learned that I can prevent hurting myself and my family by not being an alcoholic, not drinking to the point where your liver becomes bloated and extends out of your body. I had to help my sister out of a tub, and I could literally see her liver protrude from her side because of the alcoholism in her body, and then she would want another drink later that night. She died on the same day my wife came down from northern California and announced her pregnancy for our firstborn. This showed me the circle of life. As one leaves, another enters. This helped complete the circle. We are all part of one.

And on it went. We journeyed through many lives, hearing stories of doors opening in unlikely places, growth through painful experience, loss and reconciliation, the discovery of great passions. Our interviewees were remarkably willing to reflect upon their lives and share with kids on a very deep and personal level, and they were especially eager to convey the wisdom they had accrued. I became fascinated by the ways people gather life lessons, particularly the turning points (or smaller moments) when something fundamental suddenly becomes clear, and after which one is never quite the same. I remembered a quote by Joseph Campbell: "What we're learning in schools is not the wisdom of life. We're learning technologies; we're getting information." What better function for a writing activity than an exploration of life's wisdom? I decided to lead my students into the writing of short memoirs about events in their lives that had taught them something they perceived as an essential lesson.

Launching an Oral History Project

Interviewing people in the community can be among the most enriching experiences you can possibly share with your students, an impetus for writing and an inspiration for life. Our interviews sometimes involved a trek to a ramshackle house on a local ranch; other times, we arranged for our subject to come to our classroom. Either way, we discovered a special connection between generations. The elders felt relaxed around the kids and opened up with stories that had long lain silent—stories about pets, fishing holes, favorite Christmas toys, and riding the waves stark naked. Our technique evolved over time, but generally we prepared questions and took turns asking them, recorded each session, and snapped a few good photographs. The earliest of our interviews were compiled (along with kids' own poetry and reflections) into a book called Dusty Windows (named by one of our sixth graders) that ended up as a two-year, two-volume labor of love. In later years, I continued the oral history project as an elective class at the private school where I currently teach. Everyone has a story to tell, and our interviews have included people of all ages; some are fairly well known and others live quiet, but nonetheless remarkable, lives. Many of the interviews are posted on my website: zacatecanyon.com.

In addition to setting the stage for the memoir writing described in this chapter, oral history is a worthwhile interdisciplinary project that yields important skills and insights. The middle school social studies curriculum encompasses some discussion about oral tradition and how the legends and knowledge of a culture are passed along from one generation to the next. Many of my students seemed to understand intuitively that when they interviewed older people they were being entrusted with treasured memories that might otherwise be lost; they saw this as a privilege and duty, and they took it seriously. Other benefits of the project included practice in developing and asking questions; learning to listen; organizing information; expressing feelings and reflections in writing; overcoming one's shyness in order to relate to an older person; gaining a deeper sense of connection to the area called home; and becoming involved in the craft and creation of a book.

The logical first step in launching such a project is to decide on your interviewees. We initially chose local old-timers, people who had grown up in the rural area in which our school was nestled, and we focused our questions on what life was like in days gone by. Afterward, our students wrote poems and impressions about the experience. "I like to talk to the old timers because they have a lot of spirit in their hearts and souls, and they give you good advice," reflected Arianna. Olive mused, "It is almost like sitting at a campfire and hearing beautiful tales." Eduardo summed it up like this: "Talking to the elders made history come alive."

In time we realized that our subjects did not have to be old. I subsequently led a project in which we interviewed people (of any age) specifically about the work they did—these ranged from cowboy to computer technician, cashier to Congresswoman, just to name an alliterative few. There are many themes around which to organize interviews—or no particular theme at all. Tales emerge and wisdom is offered; individual personalities and experiences are manifest, but patterns appear as well. It isn't difficult to come up with names of people to talk to—invite students to make suggestions, or just ask around; you will be amazed at how this snowballs. Our oral history project became ever more inclusive over time; to this day I cannot meet an interesting person (and they seem to be everywhere) without wondering if they might agree to be interviewed.

The next phase of preparation is basically an etiquette lesson. I usually made the initial phone contact followed by a letter more formally explaining the project and establishing the date, place, and time. However, students were required to send thank-you notes afterward, along with a copy of the write-up. (More about the write-up in a minute.) Prior to the day of the interview, I always asked the students to think of a little gift to bring, or we came up with something together. Usually someone would make a commitment to bake a batch of cookies or gather some flowers, or maybe I would bring a photo of the class . . . these kinds of gestures make a huge difference. Model graciousness. Remind kids to be kind, courteous, and polite throughout the interview.

Formulate questions ahead of time. It is essential to come prepared. We asked people questions along the lines of what they enjoyed doing as children, whether they had a special place they liked to go, and what changes they had observed in our community. We found that some questions were better than others for triggering interesting memories and images. It helps to be specific, such as "What was Christmas morning like?" or "What was the wettest year you can remember?" But we always made a point at the end of asking what advice our interviewee might have for young people. We found that some of our visitors were natural storytellers and others required a bit more patience. A few started out cautiously and seemed to open up before our eyes. Be prepared for some surprises.

For the interview itself, bring pencils and paper for occasional notes, a tape recorder, and a camera. Test all equipment before you start out! Each student can choose a question or two that he or she wants to ask, and they should write these down just in case they get nervous. I had to remind kids many times to *listen* to the response and build on it, rather than simply going through their prepared questions like a script. Often a response might elicit additional questions; this is a skill the students had to work on, and it seems a great steppingstone to becoming adept in social discourse.

I did the work of summarizing and typing up the group interviews. Now and then students (usually working in pairs) arranged to interview people on their own, and in these cases they composed their own write-ups. Sometimes they simply presented the questions and answers; other times they stitched together short quotes from the interviewee with their own subjective narrative and description. (I provided some opportunity for kids to practice this skill early on by asking them to interview each other and then write a little article about their fellow student using the information acquired through the interview.) As the interviews were completed, we scanned in photos (including some very old ones that our subjects entrusted to us), made copies, and bound our little books together with plastic spirals. We distributed them to local historical agencies and libraries and placed some in a neighborhood bookstore where they sold briskly and made us briefly famous. Eventually I simplified the whole process by putting down my compulsive pencil and placing all my faith in the tiny little tape recorder, single-handedly typing up transcripts unadorned with commentary, and then posting the interviewees' own words on the website previously mentioned. These speak for themselves. Most important, the students were full participants in the actual interviews, essentially directing the course of conversation and in the process connecting with lives beyond their usual spheres.

There is a poem by Edward Arlington Robinson called "An Old Story" that concludes with these sad words: *I never knew the worth of him/ until he died.* And it is an old story indeed, one that I have learned painfully and well. Taking time to listen to the life experiences of other people is a sure way to appreciate their value and uniqueness while they still walk among us. It fosters a kind of respect and awareness that feeds into character and compassion, and these are long-term benefits. As for me, I've come to believe that there is no such thing as an ordinary life. But does this have anything to do with writing? You *bet* it does.

Preliminary Writing Activities

As you can see in the three examples provided at the start of this chapter, the interviews provide a good reference point and inspiration for seeking out life lessons. In order to provide additional models, we also read several age-appropriate essays and short stories in which a young protagonist undergoes a life-changing understanding. Excellent choices include "You Can't Just Walk on By" by Borden Deal, "Miss Awful" by Arthur Cavanaugh, and "Christmas" by Floyd Dell, all three of which happen to be anthologized in an old textbook called *Elements of Literature* that I found on a bookshelf in my classroom. Once you start looking around on your own with this theme in mind, you will discover that your choices are abundant.

Our follow-up discussions focused on what we believed the character had learned from the experience described in the story. Interpretations of what had unfolded often differed, and the lesson learned was sometimes ambiguous, as is certainly true in life. In guided discussion, students were encouraged to seek parallels in their own lives and reflect upon how they would react in similar situations.

Next, to help lead the students from other people's writing to their own, I decided to start with some poetry activities. The first—*snapshot poetry*—simply requires each student to bring in a snapshot or artifact and then write about the memories it triggers. This helped the kids to go back in time to recall sensory and emotional details from the past that might have otherwise eluded them.

The following snapshot poem by Lenora (a truly gifted sixth-grade writer) demonstrates how a photograph helped her to remember a special day in her life in precise detail, right down to the way her newly washed hair left a wet spot on her pajamas!

MY PIG AND I

My hands are hot and moist,
small and pink, holding the white telephone.
My tangled hair leaves a wet spot on my pajamas.
I feel out of place here, in this messy black and white house,
my first time away from home,
only a small pink pig to accompany me.
But we have a new friend, and as I listen quietly,
my mom tells me that I will meet my friend tomorrow,
after I go home.
I picture my mom in a bare, soap opera room, smiling.
I am charged with energy now,
like tomorrow is Christmas, and I'll get all the presents.
Tomorrow my life starts over, because I'll meet my sister.

For a second preliminary activity (suggested by my friend Bob Isaacson, who teaches writing at a local community college, and I think *he* got this idea at a poetry workshop . . . it's hard to trace these things) we first read the following poem by Yehuda Amichai:

When I Was a Child

When I was a child
grasses and masts stood at the seashore
and as I lay there
I thought they were all the same
because all of them rose into the sky above me.

Only my mother's words went with me
like a sandwich wrapped in rustling wax paper,
and I didn't know when my father would come back
because there was another forest beyond the clearing.

Everything stretched out a hand,
a bull gored the sun with its horns,
and in the nights the lights of the streets caressed
my cheeks along with the walls,
and the moon, like a large pitcher, leaned over
and watered my thirsty sleep.

While they were still under the spell of Amichai's poem, I instructed the students to begin a poem with the words: "When I was a child. . . ." followed by perceptions and illusions held in childhood. For those in need of more structure, they could follow the framework suggested by the poem:

When I was a child
I thought
I didn't know
Everything
In the nights

I thought that asking my students to recall their own childhood impressions in a poem might emphasize by contrast the wisdom that had accrued in their lives—even by sixth grade. I also hoped that the exercise would evoke memories of specific events that might have shattered an illusion, confirmed an intuitive belief, or yielded a fundamental insight; this would be material for the essay I had in mind.

My students were a particularly verbal and candid group, and they openly objected to this assignment. "When I was a child?" one groaned, "Cynthia, we're *still* children. We don't have that much stuff to look back on." I had to admit they were right, but I suggested that they focus on who they were at four or five years old, and they did their best. Here is Rebecca's:

When I was a child,
Imagination ruled my world,
And my best friend was invisible.
I thought that rainbows brought magic
And birds accompanied the earth in song.
I did not know that the world was spinning

Or why the sky was blue,
Why the grass was green
And was it really greener in the neighbor's yard?
Everything made sense to me.
I had a dog, two cats, and a family,
All walking the road of life,
Holding both my hands.
In the nights, coyotes howled.
Crickets and frogs sang lullabies,
And the moonbeams were my blanket
As I floated out to the stars.

Rebecca describes an enchanted childhood in which she felt completely safe to enjoy frog lullabies and moonbeams. But to me, her statement that "everything made sense to me" implies that it no longer does. To go from a vague inference to a full-blown anecdote is quite a leap, but I wanted the kids to mine their memory banks for something rich with learning that had taken them from this early childhood awareness to the more complex present.

In fact, I wanted the kids to seek out an epiphany—a pretty tall order, I admit—and write a short memoir about how it had happened. (Conversely, they could come up with a memory first, and *then* observe what it taught them and why it has significance. This turned out to be the best approach, as you will see.) This ambitious and abstract epiphany business might arguably be a more suitable task for high school students, but here is how I ease into it with my middle school kids—who should never be underestimated.

Epiphany

For several weeks, we have been reading and talking about epiphanies or turning points—in literature, history, and personal life. I explain that the term *epiphany* has its origin in the Christian religion, but it has come to refer to a sudden insight into the reality or essential meaning of something, often initiated by a seemingly simple occurrence or commonplace experience. In one story we read ("You Can't Just Walk on By" by Borden Deal), an encounter with a snake helps a young man to realize how precious life is. In another story ("Miss Awful" by Arthur Cavanaugh), a terribly strict and harsh teacher turns out to be a deeply caring one, and one of her students discovers a way to let her know that her life has made a difference for him.

I acknowledge to the kids what some of them have already pointed out to me: that they are not old enough to have had a great many life-changing revelations. However, I remind them that they have already written poems about what they used to believe when they were little (1), as opposed to what they now know to be true (2), and that the experience that led them from 1 to 2 may have comprised a turning point or epiphany. I suggest that they think of epiphany as an event that helped them to learn something important or see something more clearly, perhaps something that made them grow up a little. (Forgive me if I use the term *epiphany* too lightly. It happens to be a word and concept that I love.) I give the kids a little space by telling them that although *epiphany* is a powerful, filled-with-light kind of word, *their* epiphany need not be huge and dramatic. Perhaps there was a time when they first began to get a sense of how much either of their parents loved them. Or maybe an experience with an early playmate taught them something fundamental about friendship. One of *my* earliest revelations had to do with reading—I remember sitting under an oak tree on a summer day reading a novel called *Jane Eyre*. I lost all track of time and became completely immersed in the story. I realized suddenly that reading a book could literally expand my life by transporting me to another time and place. I saw that it was a wonderful escape that would be available to me always—a delightful epiphany, indeed.

I mention to the class that while we read the stories that authors have written we sometimes fail to realize that we have stories of our own. We live these stories, and we learn from them. Sometimes we do not even realize until much later what exactly it was that we learned from an experience that made it so important, but the writing and telling of it as a story may render its meaning clear. As an example, I tell the students a true tale of my own about the time I saw my eccentric uncle being treated harshly, watched his skin blanch and his lip quiver, and decided that it was better to go through life trying to be kind, even if it was not always as honest. Or I describe how at age fourteen I learned that even when someone—specifically a good-looking and shallow young man named Stanley—hurt and disappointed me, I could still go home, read a good book, eat a generous serving of ice cream, and watch a rainstorm from my bedroom window, and there's a lot of power in that. These stories inevitably trigger connections for the students, and they raise their hands, eager to tell anecdotes of their own. We allow plenty of time for this informal verbal sharing. For most of them, it's easier to talk than write, and they do not yet realize that their little vignettes are great material for memoir. So I delicately mention two other insights: One, although writing about feelings cannot heal or change them, in some inexplicable way, it helps. And two, writing casts a beam of light upon experience, making it brighter, clearer, and more meaningful.

The following is the writing task I assign to my students. I allow them time to get started in class with preliminary clusters and ideas, but this is essentially a homework assignment. Notice that I do not include a specific required length. It really depends upon the story they choose to tell, and by now they know that I probably anticipate at least a few paragraphs! I will write comments and suggestions on their first typed draft and expect a final version about two weeks from today:

AN EPIPHANY ESSAY

Your task is to write an essay that describes a particular event in your life that changed you in some way or helped you to better understand something about yourself, someone you know, or the ways of the world.

An important goal will be to present the event in a way that makes it interesting to your readers, so keep those readers in mind. How do you want them to react? What do you want them to feel or think?

Focus on the event. In other words, *show, don't tell.*

Here are some elements I will look for when I evaluate this essay:

Your *choice*: It works best if you keep things simple and choose a specific experience that did not take more than a few hours or perhaps a day. The important thing will be to make your reader clearly see how or why the experience constituted a kind of epiphany, turning point, revelation, or coming of age in your life.

Your *presentation*: Try to paint a clear picture of what happened. Make it come alive for your readers by using carefully chosen words, multisensory images, and maybe even some dialogue.

Your *care*: Pay attention to sentence structure and try to avoid distracting errors in spelling, grammar, and usage. Please edit your work; it helps to have another pair of eyeballs look it over before you turn it in.

Next, to help lead the kids deep into the recesses of memory, I suggest they answer the following questions before beginning; this is essentially a guided prewriting activity.

1. First, jot down some possible events or experiences from your life that you think may have changed you or taught you something. Narrow these down to topics that you can present in an interesting way to your readers, and then choose one event to write about. Describe this event in a few words, and see if you can express how it represents an epiphany to you. In other words, what are you going to show you have learned or realized?

2. Make a quick list of any feelings, emotions, or reactions that you experienced when this event occurred or that you feel when you are thinking about it. Write these down quickly; don't think about them too much right now.

3. Now close your eyes and try to picture in your mind what happened, allowing yourself to imagine the experience in great detail. Write down the sights, sounds, smells, and other sensory memories that come to you, even if you're not sure that the memories are accurate.

4. Note the names of anyone else who was involved in this particular event. What role did they play? Write brief descriptions of these people, including any specific words, facial expressions, or physical gestures that come to mind.

5. Consider the time sequence of this event and map out the steps and stages in which it unfolded. If it involved a conflict or problem, tell how this was resolved.

6. Finally, what epiphany or realization did this experience yield? How are you different as a result? What life lesson, large or small, did you learn? What are your feelings about the experience today?

Reflections

Reading the world—understanding life's lessons—is a retroactive process at best. Experience needs to be processed and articulated for its full meaning to be understood, and later, reading the *word* may yield surprises. In her exquisite book *I Could Tell You Stories*, Patricia Hampl writes:

> It still comes as a shock to realize that I don't write what I know, but in order to find out what I know . . . if I approach writing from memory with the assumption that I know what I wish to say, I assume that intentionality is running the show. Things are not that simple.

Hampl talks of memoir as a kind of travel writing in which the writer is not so much a survivor with a tale to tell as a pilgrim who seeks and wonders. In this spirit, I revisited a memoir of my own from a long-ago time. I had always considered my twenties a wasted decade spent dropping out of school, traveling aimlessly, and leaving various jobs and relationships. It all seemed senseless and unworthy of recollection, but my writing enabled me years later to revisit the distillation of remembered events and find their substance in the bottom of the cup. The following passage about a ride on a Greyhound bus in the early 1970s seemed to describe an epiphany, though its meaning was unclear:

> The rain had freckled all the windows and smeared the passing lights. I leaned my head against the cool glass, feeling the vibration, enjoying the sense of passivity and motion. I was getting drowsy, but I loved the knowledge that even as I rested I was moving. To the mournful beat of the wipers and the timbre of the engine, I gradually slipped into sleep. We were a ship of dreamers and desperadoes sailing through the night. I might entertain a million possibilities before dawn. I was free of love, free of the ruckus of the whole gaudy decade. Time was rushing by like a noisy parade, but I had escaped the din, pressed the button that said pause. I had no idea where I would get off, or who I would be when I did. There was only a delicious limbo, like the moment before waking, when dreams mix with morning, when all chances are good and anything might still happen; you have only to choose and make a move but don't.

Writing unearths insights that transcend the contexts in which the act of writing takes place. Reading this paragraph decades later, I see that it contains a great deal of information I didn't know was in there. Songwriter-musician Jackson Browne mused about this dimension of writing when he observed in an interview, "The writing process is all about trying to get to the truth of something and then in the end the song reflects that search for what you really think. You could surprise yourself. It can mean much more than you think it means even when you write it. This may sound like cheating, but I actually find new meanings in my songs having lived longer now. I'm in my fifties, and some of the things I said that were true, are now true in a different way, even more true."

Having lived longer now, I too can read new truths in the things I have written. I see that the bus ride described in that journal passage was not only a specific experience, but also a metaphor for the way I navigated through a certain phase of my life. I understand that the young woman who thought she was postponing life was simply living a different *kind* of life—one defined by its deliberate lack of commitment, essentially a bus ride headed nowhere in particular. Maybe she required a longer look from the sidelines before committing to a course, but in any case—to use a worn but fitting phrase—the journey was the destination. I have newfound compassion for the girl I was back then and I forgive her for all that time I thought was wasted.

But can I get all this from one muddled paragraph? Is it too much of a stretch? I think not, for in a sense, my saying so makes it so—and my remembering something means that for me, it has significance. I guess there is a narcissistic element to all this self-analysis, but memoir is such a vast, rich field to plough, I cannot overemphasize its value. By its very nature, memoir writing encourages students to discover and explore revelations about themselves and the world.

Outcomes

The wondrous thing about writing is that you never know where it will take you. Initially I had assumed that the logical approach to "epiphany writing" would be for the students to first think of the life lesson and backtrack into the story, but I had the process reversed. In most cases it was only after the memoir had been written that the lesson became known, and often I had to guide the writer into articulating the lesson by asking what the event had taught her, or how it had changed her understanding of the world. The knowledge was there, but the revelation was not explicit, and the singular experience did not yet appear to represent a general theme or principle.

This is consistent with the research of James Moffett, who wrote:

Memories and investigations represent materials both inside and outside, wealthy positions, a source of plenty . . . [The] wrong-headed strategy comes from working too deductively, starting students at high-level abstract topics, or generalities, and then asking them to go down . . . I try to get my students . . . to think about what is generic in their personal experience. I ask them to choose a personal incident in their life, something interesting, and then to write about it. Then I ask, "Of what is this incident a metaphor?" Maybe nothing will come, but when it does, you are on the road to an essay. Of what is this personal incident a metaphor? Or an emblem or symbol? What does it represent? Of what is it a token? As soon as you begin writing about types, through the tokens, through the particulars, you are dealing with what essay essentially consists of, which is coordinating an idea with an incident or instance.

Jack Phraener, a well-known instructor at the South Coast Writing Project, has a simpler way of saying it: "Recall a vivid scene from your life, describe it, then try to penetrate its meaning, the *so what* of the experience."

Sample student essays and excerpts follow. If the life lesson was not explicitly stated, I sought clarification from the student; the questions I asked are in italics. Please don't assume that these are all unusually talented kids— they aren't. The assignment simply yielded student writing that was richer and more personal than usual. I have included comments with some of the essays to show how I helped the writer back-pedal toward the real import of the experience. I wonder now if I was a bit heavy-handed about asking kids to spell it out. Brett's essay, for example, and our ensuing dialogue, provides a case for leaving well enough alone. He probably did not need me to insist that he tell when he had already so eloquently shown. Brett had looked closely at a profound moment in his life and written down the story . . . that's when the door to the inner room unlocks.

BRETT'S EXPERIENCE

When we got to the gravestone, our spirits dropped. Patriotic music started playing in my head. It was like a song you would hear at a funeral for someone important. I felt like we were at a funeral, but we weren't. I looked at my dad and I noticed that he was crying. I had never seen him cry before. I knew if he was crying he must have been heartbroken.

I went up and gave my dad a comforting hug. While I was hugging him, I could feel the warmth travel from me to him. When I was finished hugging my dad, we hopped back into the car. The car was an old Buick. I remember it felt like we were in a black and white movie.

To this day, I haven't heard anymore about this. It is like a distant memory. It felt like this moment had floated away in a balloon off to somebody else. I do believe my dad thinks about it sometimes, but I think he is trying to put it away.

When I read this, I thought that maybe Brett had recognized in this moment his father's vulnerability. This is a very big revelation for a child. Maybe he also learned that he had the ability to comfort his father. But this was not Brett's conclusion. When I asked him to try to think about the lesson of this experience, he added the following:

From this experience, I learned two things. One is that everybody has something good about them. I've learned that everybody is good at something and to cherish and become good at your one thing. The second thing I learned is to look on the bright side of things and give people the benefit of the doubt. This is good because it shows what kind of person you really are.

I never could quite see how the experience Brett described led him to those particular conclusions. He is a remarkably good-natured boy, and I had no doubt these are his sincere beliefs. But unless there is a missing piece to the story, I suspect that he was trying to fulfill my expectations and force some kind of positive lesson out of the event. I still believe this event was very significant to Brett and deepened his understanding of his father in a fundamental way. Sometimes the wisdom is in there, but cannot be explicitly articulated.

In the following sample, Lorena describes a frightening moment that unexpectedly left her with an enduring new sense of faith and security:

LORENA'S EPIPHANY

The bleachers were shiny and slick. Meghan reached out to tag me. Suddenly my foot slipped off the edge and I fell. It all happened so fast! The distant voices of the kids, the sound of bouncing balls and laughter, all faded away. And then, for a silent moment, I felt a safe feeling, holding me tight from danger, reaching out to help me.

I was sitting on the ground, not hurt at all. No one had seen me fall but my two friends. It gave me a caring feeling, like a hug from someone special, or a bright summer day. I had someone protecting me. It was a touch of love, a touch of a soft, smooth, light hand. Even if I could not see it, even if I could not hear it.

I still believe that something or someone was a guardian angel who is always by my side, watching every move I make, everything I do. They, whoever they are, keep me safe and warm as a blanket. They are there for me. I feel the strength to do anything. I am free like a bird. I am hidden from harm. Life will go on. It's like a candle that will never stop burning, and so is my love.

Nick, on the other hand, learned one of life's most painful lessons. I smiled as I read his colorful commentary about old people; then there is a shift in mood and he reflects honestly about his denial and subsequent sense of loss and regret. I think this is a very touching piece of writing:

Nick's Realization

My grandpa had had cancer for quite a while, so I pretty much forgot about it. It was easy to forget because he never showed it. He was a very happy person, although he was troubled at what people do today. He thought that trendiness was like a plague that was spreading throughout the country, taking people away from their real lives by making them believe that if you buy this or do this you will be cool. Like me, my grandpa hated brand names and the really short skirts and baggy pants and all the stupid things people do to seem hip. I really liked him. He wore checkered golf shirts, pants that were short on him, and you could see his ankles, and most of the time he wore loafers. Personally, I love old people. I think it is so cool when you see an old grandma who is as tall as you are wearing a pink hat and walking down the street with a walker moving as slow as possible to make everybody mad. My grandpa was old enough not to care what people thought of him.

I realized after my grandpa died that I hadn't spent enough time with him. I always had something better to do if he wanted to do something with me. I also learned that people do die. I never really thought it would happen because I just hate to think about it so I block it out of my head. Then, when it does happen, it is such a shock. I always get so close to people that I can't let them go. I knew this was a big part of my life. I finally knew what it was like to lose someone. I never said I wanted to.

Of course there are also happier revelations in the life of a child. I enjoyed the following description by Arielle of the momentous family gathering during which she learned to ride a bicycle:

ARIELLE'S ACCOMPLISHMENT

On the last day, we had a barbecue. It was about 5:00 and the sun had not yet set, and the last light glowed orange over everything. All my older cousins and second cousins were having a soccer game. All the parents were laughing and talking around the smoky grill. My grandpa cursed as he pulled a burnt chicken wing out of the burning coals. My great aunt told Erin and I that we were her "special helpers" so we got the red checkered tablecloth down to the old splintered table. When we were done, Erin ran to join the soccer game. I decided to try to ride that bike one more time.

I got Erin's helmet, and hopped on the bike. I gripped the handles with my sweaty hands as though I would never let go. I pushed off and again slowly pedaled, my arms tensing all their muscles with anger and frustration, and I kept the handle bars from swerving. I pedaled again, and again! Down the tiny hill I sped. I could see all the scenery flash by, and I was so happy! I had done it!

What did you learn from this experience, Arielle?

I learned how to ride a bicycle.

Did this change the way you see yourself? And is there any lesson here that you can apply to life in general?

I felt much more grown up after I learned to ride the bike. I felt I was as good as Erin. I learned that I could do something that I never thought I could do. I feel now that if I try really hard and practice, I can do almost anything!

Finally, we come to Thomas, whose life lesson was not what I expected, but based on his experience, it was the truth. I don't know why I like this piece so much; I guess it's because the descriptions are so evocative, the dialog so skillful, and the voice . . . simply *genuine*:

WHAT THOMAS LEARNED

We walked over to the office, but very slowly. It was a hot day when all of the grass on the field was dead and everything was dry, and your fingers felt like sandpaper. We had been sent to the office a million times, so we didn't really care anymore. It was just the fact that John, a teacher who used to be our good friend, was the one who was sending us.

When we got to the office, it smelled like sweet hand lotion, a grandma smell. We all three sat where we couldn't see each other because we would mess around.

"It seems you boys get in trouble a lot. You do want to graduate; don't you?" asked Esther, the principal.

"Yes," we mumbled back.

"Well, I suggest you stop getting in trouble then!" she said. She wasn't the type of principal who screamed and got really mad. She was the kind who didn't yell, but her voice had a low and maddening edge to it that sometimes seemed worse than yelling and screaming.

We were used to this routine and we didn't really care anymore, so she gave us the same old lecture and we left the office ten minutes before school was out. We were feeling hot and angry. We took some carrots from some other kids and sat under the shed, the only place where there was some shade. When the P.E. class was out, we waited for John to come and talk to us.

"Hey, you guys better stop getting in trouble or else you won't graduate," said John.

"I don't know if you have figured this out yet, John, but WE DON'T CARE! You know something, John? You used to be a lot cooler, and you used to be our friend."

"Not anymore, you guys," John replied.

I love your description of going to the office, Thomas. This is a great story, but could you please add what you've learned from this event?

I learned something from this, and that is that you can't try to make a teacher your friend. You can be friendly with a teacher, but you can't be their friend. Almost every single one of those times when we went to the office, I didn't feel that we did anything bad except the first time. But with teachers, once you do something bad, they've got their eye on you. I still feel mad about this because John was our friend up until fifth grade, and then it seemed like he turned on us. I think that part of it was our fault, but part of it was his fault, too.

I like to think that the kids assimilated yet another lesson from their epiphany essays: the idea that writing can be a process of discovery. When students closely examine events in their own lives in order to write about them, they imbue these experiences with meaning and perceive the meaning they didn't know was there. They are beginning a more conscious journey through their own stories, and I can think of no greater adventure.

6 Coming Full Circle
Assessment and Sharing

For never anything can be amiss when simpleness and duty tender it.

— WILLIAM SHAKESPEARE

When I was in sixth grade, we wrote compositions. No matter how indifferent we might be to the topic—Arbor Day, Good Manners, or the Highlight of My Summer—Miss Kennedy expected us to produce at least four decent paragraphs about it. We were never explicitly told the criteria for excellence, but correct grammar and spelling were apparently important, and it was helpful to have good penmanship. Packaging made a difference, too: a construction-paper cover with a colorful illustration and a neatly stenciled title could definitely bump you up a notch. I became a master at dutifully assembling thematic paragraphs along the blue lines of the loose-leaf page. Miss Kennedy would return our work a day or two later garnished with a letter grade written confidently in red ink. Sometimes an exclamatory word or phrase would provide further illumination: Good effort! Needs Improvement! Outstanding!

To this day, I marvel at Miss Kennedy's certainty, even envy it. How did she manage to so efficiently distill all her responses into a letter grade? Didn't the ambiguity of this task torment her? Wasn't she ever racked with doubt? Why did one composition rate a triumphant A while another was only a C? Did Loretta Chung, whose family spoke only Chinese, get any special mercy? What about Ivan, whose cursive was illegible, no matter how hard he tried?

What about the kid who wrote something strikingly creative and original but couldn't (or wouldn't) stretch it out to fill four paragraphs? Or the one who made a genuine effort but was unable to meet or even envision the particular expectations Miss Kennedy had in her head? Furthermore, after ten years of teaching, no one can tell me that the papers Miss Kennedy read wearily on Sunday night received the same attention as the ones she'd looked at over tea on Saturday morning.

Too many variables come into play here. Assessing student writing is simply not a crisp and objective procedure. Frankly, I dread it, and I know many English teachers who feel the same way. We don't deal with right or wrong answers but rather a complex gestalt, and it's hard not to agonize about each student offering. It is a process that is time-consuming, frustrating, and imprecise. (I have often suspected that the daunting task of reading and assessing student work is the reason some teachers do not give substantial writing assignments.) As one who lacks Miss Kennedy's confidence, I frequently have second thoughts and change a grade. Or I resort to giving two grades. Or I give no grade and many comments, and while I personally think that's much more meaningful, it never fails to disappoint my grade-obsessed students, all of whom have grown up in a culture that focuses on goal rather than process.

Don't Go It Alone

In order to alleviate some of the loneliness and unmitigated subjectivity of the grading process, I urge you sit down with other teachers to discuss and compare appraisals of actual student work. Maybe your school has such a process in place already; if not, be the one who initiates it. There are many ways to approach such a gathering in terms of participants, protocol, and degree of formality. It certainly isn't the ultimate solution, but it can be a helpful and enlightening exercise, and it does put things in perspective. Are you expecting too much . . . or not aiming high enough? How would someone else respond to the essay you just judged as B–? What does "good" student writing look like, anyway?

I began my teaching career at a small rural K–8 school with one main teacher per grade level. The advent of state-issued standards was yet to come, but our school community was already aware of a need to clarify expectations and set measurable goals for students as they progressed through the grades. To help develop realistic and age-appropriate writing standards, we decided to ask every child in grades 2 through 8 to respond to two out of three identical writing prompts. Students could write about a favorite sport or activity, an exciting life event, or a place they would like to visit on vacation. The prompts were administered on two different occasions, and the kids were allowed thirty minutes to write each time. The resulting writing samples were subsequently ranked by the entire faculty (and parent representatives from our curriculum council) as being either below, above, or at standard for each grade level. I know: it sounds medicinal and maybe even spiritually inconsistent with everything else in this book, but I'm just giving you the facts. It's a practical strategy and it yields a tool.

The rankings we came up with were fairly holistic and discussion based, and the process was time-consuming. The benefit was a clearer and more consistent understanding of our school's aims and expectations at each grade level—along with a glimpse of how these meshed with the reality of what students actually wrote. For me, it was also fascinating to finally find out how other teachers might evaluate the kind of student work I had been seeing. (As I said, I'm much more insecure about my own judgment than Miss Kennedy was about hers.) I enjoyed having someone else validate my disenchantment or point out attributes I might have overlooked.

The question, however, remained: what exactly do we mean by *standard* or *above standard*? It was especially hard at times to find any samples that seemed "above" standard; I think a few were ranked as such only because they were being viewed relative to others that were even more disappointing. I concluded that this was rather like grading on the curve, in that each sample was viewed not only individually but largely in relation to the others. So the value was not so much that it gave us an ideal, but rather that it provided an authentic snapshot of what we had to work with. We ultimately compiled a booklet that included an "above standard" and a "standard" writing sample for each grade level. (In addition to reproducing these in their original thirty-minute draft incarnations, we included typed or rewritten final versions to demonstrate the improvement from first cut to "publication.") These models of actual student work provided tangible examples for students, gave parents a sense of what could reasonably be expected from their children, and aided teachers in assessment.

But from whence does the ideal, uncompromised, emerge? For your students, it is most likely found in the literature you share with them. Expose them to precision, to the pleasure of what E. B. White described as "sentences turned out just right, their little hats jauntily set." Let them see what an essay looks like when it comes together in all its power and eloquence. In other words, go *beyond* standards—offer models and inspiration. This is obviously not an expectation for kids, but rather a point to which they can aspire. As teachers of writing, we must maintain an overall awareness of correctness and quality and an uncompromised sense of the ideal but temper it during assessment based on the realistic capabilities of children at each stage. We also need to factor in an element of what we know about the individual student writer, reflecting essential values such as effort. The distinction here is that you aren't just grading the product but the process as well.

And now there *are* those official state standards to tell us that at grade 6, for example, a student should be able to "use a variety of effective and coherent organizational patterns, including comparison and contrast; organization by categories; and arrangement by spatial order, order of importance, or climactic order." H-m-m-m. Does that language sound a little stilted? I think that's what happens when one seeks to describe something very complex in too prescriptive and formulaic a tone. Writing is so much more than the sum of its parts. On the other hand, you have to respect such an ambitious effort. Think of it as an attempt to chart out a lush and layered landscape as a quick summary of characteristics. What it yields at best is a collection of moderately useful milestones for teachers to keep in mind when creating assignments and developing assessment criteria, and that's not bad. But remember, *you* are the teacher. Look beyond those lists as you lead the students into the real experience and exploration of that vast territory.

The Rubric

And so the teachers and parents at my old school spent several weeks reading student essays and discussing goals and standards, but we still didn't have a consensus on how an individual paper should be graded. Thus came the rubric: a score sheet that attempts to quantify that which is not by nature quantifiable. A good rubric renders the evaluation tangible, crisp, and useful; it's a practical tool for both teachers and students. The performance indicators outlined in those state-adopted standards—along with everything I know intuitively about writing—can be organized into the following four general components:

1. Content and Voice
2. Structure and Organization
3. Spelling, Grammar, and Usage
4. Presentation and Effort

These form the basis of the generic rubric presented at the end of this chapter. Students may earn 1 to 5 points per section, with a total of 17 to 20 points yielding an A, 13 to 16 a B, and so forth. It is an intentionally balanced evaluation format in which a student who is weak in spelling, for example, can make up points by showing thought and creativity, or a student who lacks creativity can compensate by having presented a work that shows effort and care. A truly outstanding piece of work, of course, would have high point values in all areas. Because writing is a process, students are encouraged to revisit, rewrite, and improve their written work based upon teacher comments and the scoring of the rubric. In my class, the improved grade on an assignment that is redone and resubmitted is calculated into the student's overall average.

Writing assessment thus becomes an important part of instruction, as all good assessment should be. But use the rubric prudently—more about this in a minute.

Variations Galore

Despite all this reflection (and maybe because of it) I continue to grapple with assessment methods and philosophies. The further I explore it, the clearer it becomes that my insecurity is reality based; there simply is no consensus about the "best" technique for grading student writing, no foolproof, easy method, no surefire, consistent way to render quantitative something so complex and subjective. I recently participated in a couple of scoring workshops to facilitate research sponsored by the National Writing Project, including three days spent applying a type of six-trait analytic scoring to hundreds of student writing samples from all over the United States. Although there was strong statistical agreement among the teachers in our carefully trained group, it is nonetheless evident that the outcome of such an approach depends upon which traits are selected, how clearly each is defined, how carefully the group is normed, and even how strongly individual scorers may favor particular traits (perhaps unconsciously). I discovered, for example, that I am very swayed by voice—by which I mean a student's engagement with the task, an element of personality, a sort of sparkle and glint, if you will. Indeed, voice is among the most interpretive and difficult of traits to define (as opposed to, say, conventions, which are generally either correct or not and therefore a very easy element to score). Anyway, you can see how quickly this gets complicated.

In another workshop, I was introduced to a method called "forced choice" or "forced comparison" scoring, in which the scorer looks at two writing samples by the same student and is literally forced to decide which is better, and how much better, holistically and in specific areas. In order to accomplish this, it's hard to avoid some hair-splitting, particularly when the two papers are virtually indistinguishable in terms of quality; in such cases a personal preference for a particular attribute can have a disproportionate effect. On the other hand, forced comparison necessitates very meticulous analysis of the work of each individual student, and there is something refreshing about comparing samples by the same student rather than measuring the work against that of other students or by contrast to a certain ideal. This approach originated with Richard Haswell, who developed it in the 1980s and called it intrapersonal scoring; in a way, it's like a mini-portfolio assessment.

Graduate student Tim Dewar, who is currently doing research in this area at the University of California at Santa Barbara, explains that many of the analytic trait-scoring methodologies came out of universities with the advent of open enrollment; schools needed practical techniques for placing students into writing classes. (Tim recommends a book called *Teaching and Assessing*

Writing by Edward White for those who wish to delve further.) Another ambitious attempt to assess student writing on a large scale transpired more recently with the addition of a high-stakes essay component to the SAT. Its six-point scoring rubric was promptly criticized for rewarding writing that is formulaic, uninspired, not necessarily factual, and as long and rambling as it can get within the twenty-five minutes allotted. The ensuing uproar once again highlights the inherent difficulties of attempting to evaluate writing, period.

Six Basic Principles

Over the years, I have had many conversations with other teachers about assessment. One talented and experienced teacher summed up it up with a sigh and this comment: "The moment we put a grade on a paper, we are ranking kids and putting them in competition with each other. It's no longer about the writing." I think she's right. But given the context of real world demands, it helps to keep some tools in your back pocket. Here then are six basic principles for a constructive approach to assessment that contributes to growth and is more than a grade.

1. *Clearly state expectations.* For longer writing assignments it is essential to prepare and distribute a detailed sheet describing the task and expectations. Directions given informally and orally tend to generate odd mutations of what you had in mind, so be specific, and whenever possible, show your students a model. (The words of a published author can provide inspiration, but seeing what other students have actually written for the same assignment is also extremely valuable.) Finally, tell your students exactly what attributes you will be looking for when you assess their work. Not only does a clear description of the assignment help them to understand what they are being asked to do, but it translates for you into a checklist for assessment.

2. *Use rubrics—but use your instinct too.* You may use a generic rubric such as the one I have included at the end of the chapter, or customize a rubric based upon a particular assignment. Some assignments might emphasize certain concrete skills—for example, use of commas, transitions, or dialogue—and the grade will be based only on these stated elements. If you plan to

use a rubric, let the students have access to it ahead of time, along with the assignment description. And remember that despite its precise and formal appearance, the rubric is still just a guideline. Use it with a healthy degree of skepticism and remember there is no scientific way to assign number values to the written word. You still need to write out comments and suggestions for your students, and ask them questions about their work.

3. *Invite the rewrite.* If you've written helpful comments, corrections, questions, and suggestions, or if the kids have offered feedback to a fellow writer, the next logical step is for the student to take these into consideration and rework the piece accordingly. If not, the process ends right there—no one is going to pay attention to anything but the letter grade, and not much is learned. Of course, many kids would rather *not* have the option to rewrite. It's much easier to turn in the work, whatever it is, feel that it's done, and never have to deal with it again. "I can live with a C–," replied Jeremy recently when I showed him how he could improve his essay. I confess I turned my invitation into a command at that point. Revision is an integral part of writing, but there's a larger message here, something about sticking with a task until it's right, working through a process, caring about the outcome. Use your discretion in how you implement this concept, but I think it's very important to allow or require rewriting in some, if not all, assignments, and then factor in the better grade and the student's willingness to make the effort. But know when to back off, also. Sometimes it's as done as it's ever going to be. Here again, listen to your instinct.

And in case you're worried, I can reassure you: grading rewrites will not spiral into an overwhelming task because it is not in the nature of most students to keep rewriting. In any event, I give a time limit for the rewrite, and in the meantime, new assignments are forthcoming. Therefore, it does not benefit a student to intentionally do a so-so job on the first final draft just because she can turn it in again. However, the option does help a student who for some reason blew it the first time . . . and it does help a student who is truly motivated to do better. How much significant revision must be demonstrated? This is not a simple, quantifiable matter. Let's put it this way: I ask for more than corrected punctuation. I ask that an authentic attempt be made to follow suggestions. The draft with my comments must be attached so that I can see the extent to which this was done.

4. *Be resourceful.* Don't carry the entire burden on your shoulders. Utilize students for peer feedback about one another's work. They might work in pairs or small groups, reading or listening and giving written comments back to the author. In particular, have them note what seemed to work well, parts that were unclear, suggestions they have, and lingering questions. (See also Helping Your Students with Revision in Chapter 3.) Require that all papers be edited and signed by a parent, sibling, or peer before they are submitted to you—it's amazing how many errors a second pair of eyeballs will catch. Your reading of it should not be the first time the work is edited. Self-assessment is another interesting and valuable technique. Distribute a rubric or questionnaire tailor-made for the particular assignment. Ask students to complete it and give themselves a grade based upon the level of effort they put into it, the degree to which they feel it succeeds, and any elements you choose to emphasize. This doesn't mean they will necessarily get the grade they bestow upon themselves, but it certainly can be a helpful factor, and it does yield insights. Some students readily sing their own praises while others are much tougher on themselves than you would ever be; most are surprisingly honest.

5. *Keep the big picture in mind.* In writing as in life, what matters most isn't where you are; it's how far you've come. Each student in my class has an accessible file folder in which to keep her completed written work. Keeping portfolios provides an overall view of what has been achieved throughout the year, allows you to monitor progress over time, and gives kids a sense of accomplishment too. Make sure you maintain a checklist of all key assignments that should be included in the portfolio. Encourage students to comment on sticky notes to highlight items they are most proud of or to reflect upon something they wish they had done differently, or invite them to re-write an earlier piece, but don't overcomplicate this. In my interpretation, the portfolio is essentially a collection of the work each student has done throughout the year, affording them the satisfaction of seeing their own progress and achievements. I assess individual assignments, not the portfolio itself, but a look at the portfolio does give me a holistic picture for each student. Near the end of the year, my students select their favorite pieces, add some new components, and compile individual books of their own work, with hand-decorated covers that reflect their tastes and personalities. The

books tell me a lot about where they are with their writing and their level of pride about what they have done; these *are* graded.

Much has been written about portfolios as an assessment tool and a learning strategy; if you want to use them in a more comprehensive way, I recommend *Portfolio Portraits* by Donald H. Graves and Bonnie S. Sunstein or *A Portfolio Primer* by Geoff Hewitt, among others.

6. *Celebrate and share.* Writing is born to be read and heard. Make time for students to read their work out loud to the class. Publish a class literary magazine to showcase their art and writing. Help your kids find real publishing opportunities, too—watch for magazine invitations, newspaper-sponsored contests, or other chances that students might overlook. Organize a coffee house–style student reading in the evening: invite parents and community members, ask the kids to dress in black, offer refreshments, play a little Miles Davis in the background as people wander in. Make it an event. Or launch a schoolwide poetry contest culminating in a springtime assembly. Writing too often goes unsung and uncelebrated. It deserves at least as much hoopla as athletics. You can view this as a part of assessment, but it is also a way of bringing the process full circle.

And Sometimes Don't Assess at All

Having dutifully talked about writing assessment, there is a larger point that ultimately needs to be made: damn it all, anyway. The most important truth is that kids need to write and write and write some more. There is never enough time to do this, but you must make a gallant effort anyway. Writing is hard, but it is a habit and a discipline, and it only comes with practice. It is a journey of creative discovery *and* the primary means by which students process knowledge and connect ideas. It is a priority of the highest order. But writing is often sacrificed because there is so much material to cover, and because— let's face it—it means more work for teachers, too. After all, whatever those kids write must eventually be read, commented on, sometimes even graded.

Sometimes graded? Sometimes. What a breakthrough it has been for me to realize that not every piece of writing requires formal assessment and a letter grade! In fact, the truth is quite the contrary. Too much focus on the grade can be a major impediment to the writing process. Students need to find their own voices, learn their feelings, and tend to their craft without always anticipating a judgment at the other end. I turn once again to the poet William Stafford for his perceptive observations on this subject:

> If a student learns to seek praise and avoid blame, the actual feel and excitement of learning and accomplishing will be slighted in favor of someone else's reaction. The student's own, inner, self-realizing relation to the materials is displaced . . . [Beginners] benefit from impulse, excitement, motion, trying out things without the menace of disapproval (or the distraction of imminent gaining of approval).

The objective of writing should not be teacher approval but rather the writing itself—the flow of words, the exploration of ideas, the pain and the pleasure. I am pragmatic enough to understand that there is correctness and convention in writing and it is my role as a teacher to make this clear in my instruction and editing. I know too that students submit work that ranges from weak to exceptional, and they deserve and expect a grade. But it is also essential that they be given ample opportunities for writing that I will read and discuss with them but to which I will never affix a grade. As Donald Murray said, "We will write nothing but garbage if we do not practice critical thinking towards the end of the writing process, but it is dangerous to be too critical too early."

For not-to-be-graded journeys into written expression, I suggest writing-workshop time during which students may write freely based entirely on their own ideas and imagination. This will not appeal to all of them: there are those who would *like* to participate but struggle for a start, and quite a few kids actually prefer more structured activities. For the latter, this is a good chance to work one-on-one or in small groups on focused skill building or writing to specific prompts. On the other hand, many students will dive into writing as though they have been waiting years for just this moment, and that's what makes my heart sing.

But rather than just handing over the time, I first ask my students to submit "proposals" so I know what they plan to work on. These need not be highly developed; I just want to hear their ideas and see evidence of some preliminary thought and motivation. To do this, they answer the following questions in an informal letter or statement to me.

1. Would you like to have writing workshop time? Why or why not?
2. What would you work on if you had writing workshop time? Please describe your idea and your goal as best you can at this point.
3. What difficulties (if any) do you anticipate?
4. Are there any other comments or thoughts you would like to share about this?

This year, three students admitted candidly right at the start that they did not want writing-workshop time. (During these periods, they worked on developing paragraphs, comparing and contrasting, various conventions, and other isolated skills that I thought would be useful to them.)

On the other side, here is a good example of an affirmative response from Joie, a sixth-grade student who was very eager for writing-workshop time:

> I am going to write about a made-up racehorse. He will race a lot and win. His name will be Young American. I will explain him as a foal and his life as he grows up. The main characters will be the trainer, the owner, the jockey, and Young American. This story will be fairly long because there is a lot to explain about a racehorse's life, but I hope to start as soon as possible. There will be no difficulties when I am writing. I love writing and I love horses.

Noli, who is a lover of words, also wanted workshop time and was hoping that her story would unfold as she wrote:

> My story is a romantic fantasy. It begins introducing Kiriya, a young-ish boy at a high school. He only sees glimpses of shy and sheltered Kitsuko, but he is insatiably curious about her. Then he learns her secret and is taken to a new and wonderful place. This is kind of sketchy, I know, but it might grow up by itself. I hope.

Colton proposed a complex tale about eight friends whose home planets are destroyed; Luke wanted to follow the adventures of a character named Telekinetic Tom; and Kyle wished to start a Depression-era story that soon led him to a Web search about prices and conditions of the 1930s and the names of towns in upstate New York. Hayley proposed a collection of bedtime stories and lobbied (in her own unique voice) for more writing time:

> I think I could do better if we had more time for writing workshop. I think this is very worthwhile because if you think about it, not many schools do free writing as often as we do, even if SOME people don't use the time well. It's like people

telling you to drink the milk out of your cereal bowl because millions of people would cut off their toe to eat like we do. We should drink that milk while we get the chance. It's the same principle, just way less desperate.

Hayley's comments reminded me that I tend to cut writing-workshop time because of the students who cannot handle it, rather than extend it because of those who *can*. Why do I give more value to the former? It's an insidious tendency that I need to watch.

By far the most frequently anticipated difficulty was fear of not being able to finish the work, but in a context that focuses on the process, completion is not essential. I ask to see only three to five typed pages of the work at the culmination of a period of about a month, and students confer with me about where it's headed. Some pieces find their way to completion while others do not. There is certainly a special sense of accomplishment and validation that comes with finishing a story, but I figure this outcome is way more likely to occur if one actually begins.

Of course, making these large blocks of time available in the face of so many competing demands requires a real commitment. You need to believe that the activity has value. My rationale is simple: *Nothing* has more value in the learning of a craft or skill than the doing of it, the practice, the pure performance. The writing workshops of recent sixth-grade classes yielded horse stories and kidnappings, several fascinating science fiction tales, a re-telling of a historical event, a collection of poems, an autobiographical memoir, three chapters of a fantasy novel, and other assorted works. Students experimented with the use of dialogue, unearthed more effective vocabulary words, played with metaphors, worked their way in and out of messes, and experienced language as a medium of creation and enjoyment.

Was any of this work actually good? Perhaps, but that was never the point. It was all about process. Better questions might be: Did the students learn anything of value? and Did they develop more positive feelings about writing? To both of these, I would offer a resounding yes.

A Basic Rubric for Essays and Creative Writing

I. Content and Voice
The work should show thought, creativity, and substance.

- The writing flows smoothly, and there is a variety of sentence structure.
- The work employs varied vocabulary and avoids repetition of words.
- It uses well-chosen words, description, detail, and literary devices such as metaphor.
- It adheres to the assigned topic and shows real engagement with the topic.
- It demonstrates background knowledge and/or research and draws upon factual context.
- Conclusions are supported by fact and anecdotal illustration.
- Overall, it conveys its theme or message effectively.

II. Structure and Organization
Readers should be able to understand and follow what the writer is communicating.

- The essay has an introduction, conclusion, and "body."
- Paragraphs are neither too short nor overlong.
- Transitions between paragraphs are smooth.
- Each paragraph has a topic sentence, supporting sentences, and conclusion.
- Work is clear and well organized overall.

III. Spelling, Grammar, and Usage
The work should be free of distracting errors in spelling, grammar, and usage.

- Spelling is correct.
- Capitalization and punctuation are correct.
- Sentences are complete; there are no fragments.
- There are no run-on sentences.
- Verb forms and tenses are correct and consistent.
- Overall, proper grammar and structure is used.

IV. Presentation and Effort
The work should show effort and care.

- It is of adequate length (depending upon assignment).
- It has a cover and title page that includes the title, student's name, and date.
- It includes an edited first draft that is attached to the back of the final draft.
- It includes a drawing or illustration (optional).
- It is neatly typed, word-processed, or handwritten in cursive using black or blue ink.
- It shows evidence of having gone through the stages of the writing process (pre-composing, draft, editing, and revision).

Scoring
Students may earn 1 to 5 points per section.

17–20 points = A	13–16 points = B
9–12 points = C	5–8 points = D

Students are welcome to revise and improve their written work based upon teacher comments and the scoring of this rubric. The improved grade on an assignment that is redone and resubmitted will be calculated into the student's overall average. (Note this means more than quick corrections.)

Bibliography

AMICHAI, YEHUDA. 1996. *The Selected Poetry of Yehuda Amichai, Newly Revised and Expanded Edition.* Berkeley: University of California Press.

ANGELOU, MAYA. 1991. *I Shall Not Be Moved.* New York: Bantam.

ATWELL, NANCIE. 1987. *In the Middle: Reading and Learning with Adolescents.* Portsmouth, NH: Boynton Cook.

———. 1998. *In the Middle: New Understandings About Writing, Reading, and Learning.* Portsmouth, NH: Heinemann.

BROWN, RITA MAE. 1988. *Starting from Scratch: A Different Kind of Writers' Manual.* New York: Bantam Books.

BROWNE, JACKSON. February 2001. Interview with Cynthia Carbone Ward and Dunn Middle School students. Gaviota, California. *http://www.zacatecanyon.com/Interviews/jbrowne.htm.*

CALIFORNIA STATE BOARD OF EDUCATION. 2005. Standards & Frameworks. "English-language Arts Content Standards." 1.3 Writing Strategies.

CAMPBELL, JOSEPH, WITH BILL MOYERS. 1988. *The Power of Myth.* New York: Doubleday.

CAREY, MICHAEL A. 1989. *Poetry: Starting from Scratch.* Lincoln, NE: Foundation Books.

CARROLL, LEWIS. 2000. *Alice's Adventures in Wonderland and Through the Looking Glass.* New York: Signet Classics (reissue edition).

CHABON, MICHAEL. 2000. *Werewolves in Their Youth and Other Stories.* New York: Picador.

CISNEROS, SANDRA. 1991. "My Name." In *The House on Mango Street.* New York: Vintage Books.

COLLINS, BILLY. 1988. "Introduction to Poetry." In *The Apple That Astonished Paris.* Fayetteville: University of Arkansas Press.

———. 2003. *Poetry 180.* New York: Random House.

CUMMINGS, E. E. 1968. *Complete Poems 1913–1962.* New York: Harcourt Brace Jovanovich.

CUTLER, JANE. 1999. *The Cello of Mr. O.* New York: Dutton Children's Books.

DEWEY, JOHN. 1951. *The Philosophy of John Dewey.* In *The Library of Living Philosophers.* Edited by Paul Arthur Schlipp. New York: Tudor Publishing.

DUNCKER, PATRICIA. "Creative Writing" article appearing on website of British Council Arts. www.britishcouncil.org/arts-literature-activities-creativewriting-intro.htm.

ELBOW, PETER. 1998. *Writing Without Teachers*. 2d ed. New York: Oxford University Press.

GOLDBERG, NATALIE. 1986. *Writing Down the Bones*. Boston: Shambhala.

GRAVES, DONALD H., AND BONNIE S. SUNSTEIN. 1992. *Portfolio Portraits*. Portsmouth, NH: Heinemann.

HAMPL, PATRICIA. 1999. *I Could Tell You Stories*. New York: W.W. Norton.

HASWELL, RICHARD. 1983. "Minimal Marking." *College English* 45 (6).

———. 2001. *Beyond Outcomes: Assessment and Instruction Within a University Writing Program*. Westport, CT: Ablex.

HEARD, GEORGIA. 1995. *Writing Toward Home: Tales and Lessons to Find Your Way*. Portsmouth, NH: Heinemann.

HEWITT, GEOFF. 1994. *A Portfolio Primer: Teaching, Collecting, and Assessing Student Writing*. Portsmouth, NH: Heinemann.

HILLOCKS, GEORGE. 1975. *Observing and Writing*. Urbana, IL: National Council of Teachers of English.

———. 1995. *Teaching Writing as Reflective Practice*. New York: Teachers College Press.

HINTON, S. E. 1967. *The Outsiders*. New York: Viking Press.

HIRSCH, EDWARD. 1999. *How to Read a Poem: And Fall in Love with Poetry*. New York: Harcourt.

JANECZKO, PAUL B. 1985. *Pocket Poems*. New York: Bradbury Press.

———. 1987. *Going Over to Your Place: Poems for Each Other*. New York: Bradbury Press.

———. 1994. *Poetry from A to Z: A Guide for Young Writers*. New York: Simon & Schuster.

JUNG, CARL, GERHARD ADLER, AND R. F. C. HULL. 1981. *The Development of Personality (Collected Works of C.G. Jung, Volume 17)*. Princeton, NJ: Bollingen.

KEILLOR, GARRISON. 2002. *Good Poems*. New York: Viking.

———. 2005. *Good Poems for Hard Times*. New York: Viking.

KOCH, KENNETH. 1974. *Rose, where did you get that red? Teaching Great Poetry to Children*. New York: Vintage Books, division of Random House.

KOONTZ, TRIXIE, DOG. 2004. *Life Is Good! Lessons in Joyful Living*. Edited by Dean Koontz. New York: Yorkville Press.

KOOSER, TED. 1980. *Sure Signs: New and Selected Poems*. Pittsburgh, PA: University of Pittsburgh Press.

———. 2005. *The Poetry Home Repair Manual: Practical Advice for Beginning Poets.* Lincoln: University of Nebraska Press.

LEAR, EDWARD. 1987. *Edward Lear's Nonsense Omnibus: With All the Original Pictures, Verses, and Stories of His Book of Nonsense, More Nonsense, Nonsense Songs, Nonsense Stories, and Alphabets.* New York: Penguin.

LEVINE, MEL. 2003. *The Myth of Laziness.* New York: Simon & Schuster.

LEVINE, MELVIN D., WITH MARTHA REED. 2001. *Developmental Variation and Learning Disorders.* Cambridge, MA and Toronto: Educators Publishing Service.

LEWIS, JENNY. 2002. "The Good That Won't Come Out." In *The Execution of All Things,* by Rilo Kiley. Los Angeles, CA: DePrecious Music.

MCCOURT, FRANK. 1999. *'Tis: A Memoir.* New York: Scribner.

MOFFETT, JAMES. 1989. "Bridges: From Personal Writing to the Formal Essay." *Center for the Study of Writing.* Berkeley: University of California.

MOYERS, BILL. 1999. *Fooling with Words: A Celebration of Poets and Their Craft.* New York: Perennial.

MURRAY, DONALD H. 1982. *Learning by Teaching: Selected Articles on Learning by Teaching.* Upper Montclair, NJ: Boynton Cook.

———. 2003. *The Craft of Revision.* 5th ed. Boston: Heinle.

NATIONAL COMMISSION ON WRITING IN AMERICA'S SCHOOLS AND COLLEGES. 2003. *The Neglected R: The Need for a Writing Revolution.* New York: College Entrance Exam Board.

NERUDA, PABLO. 1988. "The Word." In *Lines on the Line: The Testimony of Contemporary Latin American Authors.* Edited by Doris Meyer. Berkeley: University of California Press.

NORRIS, KATHLEEN. 1993. *Dakota: A Spiritual Geography.* Boston: Houghton Mifflin.

NYE, NAOMI SHIHAB. 1994. "Jerusalem." In *Red Suitcase.* Rochester, NY: BOA Editions.

———. 1998. "Morning Glory." In *Fuel.* Rochester, NY: BOA Editions.

OHANIAN, SUSAN. July/August 1986. "The Tantalizing Vagueness of Teaching." *Learning.*

OLSEN, CAROL BOOTH. 1987. *Practical Ideas for Teaching Writing as a Process.* Sacramento: California Department of Education.

PROBST, ROBERT. 2000. "Literature as Invitation." *Voices from the Middle* 8 (3): 8–15.

PYLE, HOWARD. 1986. *The Merry Adventures of Robin Hood.* New York: Signet Classics.

ROMANO, TOM. 1982. "The Teacher." *English Journal* 71 (March).

———. 1995. *Writing with Passion: Life Stories, Multiple Genres.* Portsmouth, NH: Heinemann.

Seuss, Dr. 1961. *The Sneetches and Other Stories.* New York: Random House Books for Young Readers.

Soto, Gary. 1990. *Baseball in April and Other Stories.* New York: Harcourt Brace.

Stafford, William. 1996. "Being a Person." Lewiston, ID: Confluence Press.

———. 1996. "Silver Star." In *Even in Quiet Places.* Lewiston, ID: Confluence Press.

———. 1998. *Crossing Unmarked Snow: Further Views on the Writer's Vocation.* Edited by Paul Mercant and Vincent Wixon. Ann Arbor: University of Michigan Press.

Stafford, William. 1998. *The Way It Is: New and Selected Poems.* St. Paul, MN: Graywolf Press.

Steinbeck, John. 1939. *The Grapes of Wrath.* New York: Penguin Books.

Trelease, Jim. 1993. *Read All About It! Great Read-Aloud Stories, Poems, and Newspaper Pieces for Preteens and Teens.* New York: Penguin.

Twain, Mark. [1884] (1948). *The Adventures of Huckleberry Finn.* New York: Grosset & Dunlap.

Untermeyer, Louis, ed. 1962. *Modern American Poetry.* New York: Harcourt, Brace, & World.

White, Bailey. 1993. *Mama Makes Up Her Mind: And Other Dangers of Southern Living.* Boston: Addison Wesley.

White, Edward M. 1985. *Teaching and Assessing Writing.* San Francisco: Jossey-Bass.

White, T. H. 1978. *The Sword in the Stone.* New York: Laurel Leaf.

Williams, Oscar. 1975. *Immortal Poems of the English Language: An Anthology.* New York: Pocket Books, a Division of Simon & Schuster, Inc.

Wormser, Baron, and David Cappella. 2004. *A Surge of Language: Teaching Poetry Day by Day.* Portsmouth, NH: Heinemann.

Index